Praise for *Frust*

"Katie Powell gets it. She offers bo͗ acknowledging the challenges that teachers face in a way only a veteran educator can (adding her signature humor along the way). This book provides real, usable solutions that any teacher can deploy to break through common classroom frustrations. Katie's warmth shines through in her writing style. Any educator that picks up this book will be able to feel the supportive and encouraging spirit she exudes throughout. She knows what makes students tick—and how to leverage that to the benefit of both student and teacher. Her examples are so "real life" that every teacher, especially middle school teachers, will see their own experiences reflected in this book. It's truly a must-read for every teacher. *Frustration Busters* offers essential advice for novice teachers just developing their classroom management style. And for more seasoned educators, the lecture buster activities alone are worth the price of admission."

—Stephanie Simpson, chief executive officer of the
Association for Middle Level Education

"I LOVE *Frustration Busters* and was hooked before I had finished the first page! As a school counselor, I'm well acquainted with the toll that frustration can take on a student, whether they avoid an assignment, quit as soon as it gets hard, or lose focus and poke a classmate. Of course, no teacher is immune to frustration either, whether they're tasked with too many responsibilities or clashing with a disruptive student. With her trademark authenticity, honesty and humor, Katie shares concrete ways to dive beneath surface behaviors and solve the right problem. This is the practical, compassionate, evidence-based guide every educator needs to bust frustration, preserve the teacher-student relationship, and derive more joy from their work."

—Phyllis Fagell, LCPC, author of *Middle School Matters:
The 10 Key Skills Kids Need to Thrive in Middle School
and Beyond—and How Parents Can Help*

"Katie has yet again written a book that merits space on the book-shelves of new and veteran teachers alike. Her heart for teachers is evident throughout this work as she focuses on finding ways to support teachers—knowing that will support our students. *Frustration Busters* is guided by an exhaustive amount of research to provide long-term, lasting solutions. The book is filled with purposeful anecdotes paired with practical strategies that teachers can refer to in times of need."

—Phil Strunk, teacher and moderator of Wins and Losses Chat

FRUSTRATION BUSTERS

FRUSTRATION BUSTERS

UNPACKING AND RESPONDING TO CLASSROOM MANAGEMENT CHALLENGES

Katie Powell

Frustration Busters: Unpacking and Responding to Classroom Management Challenges
© 2021 Katie Powell

This book is available at special discounts when purchased in quantity for educational purposes or for use as premiums, promotions, or fundraisers. For inquiries and details, contact the publisher at books@daveburgessconsulting.com.

Published by Dave Burgess Consulting, Inc.
San Diego, CA
DaveBurgessConsulting.com

Library of Congress Control Number: 2021947494
Paperback ISBN: 978-1-956306-03-3
Ebook ISBN: 978-1-956306-04-0

Cover and interior design by Liz Schreiter
Edited and produced by Reading List Editorial: ReadingListEditorial.com

This book is dedicated to all the educators who have shown up—even on the hard days, who have done their best to put students first, who have supported their colleagues, who have given compassion in ample measure, and have shared readily of their well-stocked candy drawers.

This book is also dedicated to those who have struggled with whether to stay in the profession, who have sat at their desks with the lights off at the end of a class and wondered if they can make it through the rest of the day, who have found themselves with compassion fatigue in real measure, and have eaten their candy drawer in its entirety.

This job isn't easy. But it's important. I sure don't have all the answers, but I know a few things:

We are better together.

It's OK to be not OK sometimes.

We'll keep trying because our students deserve the best.

CONTENTS

Introduction

Among the Doritos Crumbs and Stains That Should Not Be Named

I lay down on the floor. Right there in the hallway, amid Doritos crumbs, clumps of dirt, and the lingering stains of that which should not be named. That's how bad it was. In my dress pants and blazer, I lay prostrate right there on the floor.

It was Friday, April 26. My colleague was absent for a funeral, and no one had picked up to sub for her. Ordinarily, whoever was available on staff would have stepped in to supervise, but it was standardized test season, so literally every available adult and every available space had already been claimed. Our solution was to divvy up my colleague's students, half a dozen or so per class, and have them work on the assignments she'd left while we taught our own classes. This kind of thing happens. We roll with it.

So I got that going. And my morning went reasonably well. I got her students settled, then launched my reading groups. We even did an escape-the-underworld activity to go along with our chapter in *The Lightning Thief*. (All but one team escaped on time. I guess they're still stuck in the underworld somewhere . . .)

Just as I was patting myself on the back for how smoothly the morning had gone, one of the students from my colleague's class screamed.

Like, literally screamed.

Then banged his head against the table.

See, while I was so successfully running my reading groups, he'd been getting increasingly stressed and overwhelmed with the amount of work he had to do.

And I didn't see it.

I had him in my class later in the day, so I knew him well. I wrapped him in a hug and told him he was safe and that I was so, so sorry. He sobbed into my shoulder, and a moment later, I felt him relax. When he sat back, I apologized, looking directly into his eyes, and then worked with him to adjust the number of problems he had to do so he didn't feel so overwhelmed. He sat up straighter, grinned, and said, "I can do that!"

After my combined class dismissed, I received my afternoon class and about eight of my colleague's students (also kids I have in my morning class). I tried to repeat my routine. I mean, it worked so well the first time, right? OK, minus one meltdown. But, for the most part, not TOO bad . . .

Nope.

I got my colleague's students started, turned to my reading groups to get them going, and noticed one of the students I'd just settled walking across the chairs.

I turned back to him, redirected him, and my reading groups fell apart.

I turned back to them, got them settled, and sat down to look at my list to see which reading group was up for reteaching.

Now, I need to explain that we had been eating lunch about forty-five minutes later than usual to accommodate standardized testing. And my students' bladders are apparently trained—well—for our normal lunch time. So about the time my cheeks hit the chair, a kid asked to be excused. Then another. Before long, we had a bladder-inspired conga line going. I, in all my sixth-grade-teacher glory, said, "Looks like we have a contagious condition of pee-ness."

Yes. Yes I did.

The synapses in my brain caught on a nanosecond too late. You may think this story will end there.

It doesn't.

While I was trying desperately to redeem myself from *that*, a student messaged me over a digital service we were using in our reading groups and said he needed to tell me something. Right away. So, we messaged for a moment while I side-eyed the other reading groups and the students working on my colleague's assignment.

Another student had a Juul. You know, the super small, super hard-to-catch electronic cigarette that vaporizes cartridges of highly suspect and highly addictive substances.

Did I mention I teach sixth grade?

I did some super fast sleuthing to try to gather more information about the Juul situation, emailed a "HELP ME" to the appropriate admin, and then went back to juggling classes.

The ensuing disciplinary inquiries and action wound up involving multiple students.

Who cried.

Which made their friends cry.

While I was trying to run reading groups.

And supervise my colleague's students.

And keep one from climbing the chairs.

And keep the girls from using the bathroom, no matter how much their bladders wanted to conga, because the bathroom had been closed temporarily as our administration reviewed the cameras to try to get to the bottom of who may have used a Juul in there.

Did I mention that students from both classes were returning at random intervals after finishing that standardized test?

And that I had to get each one started on their work.

While running reading groups.

And supervising my colleague's students.

And keeping the student off the chairs.

While 6,412 students were crying.

And apparently that Juul had been hidden somewhere in my room.

And I had an escape room planned?

A student called me over and said, "I bet this is one of the weirder Fridays you've ever had."

Y'all.

When the bell rang, two students who had been too tearful to finish the work stayed with me, and we walked through it together.

Another came in and said all the crying had triggered a memory of her own traumatic experience, and she was in tears too. So, I tried out a strategy I had just read about the night before and had her sit and read aloud to me. The premise is that you can't think about what's upsetting you AND read aloud at the same time. It safely got her mind off things so she could calm down and move on.

By the time I dismissed all three students, thirty-five minutes into my fifty-five-minute prep period, I was ready to collapse.

So I did. Right in the hallway, on that floor, among the crumbs and suspect smells. My colleagues stood around me, shoes near my head and shoulders, and just chuckled and shook their heads.

We'd all been there.

Well, maybe not literally *there*, but you get what I mean. We all know that feeling.

I was left with a feeling of defeat I can't quite describe. I had planned every aspect of my lesson. It was going to be stellar. I was so excited about that escape room. But no amount of planning could have prepared me for what unfolded that day. I had failed for reasons that felt so far out of my control.

Even after the dismissal bell, I couldn't shake that feeling of discouragement. As I sat at the small-group table in my then empty and quiet classroom, I got a text from my husband that my son had been held after school for not completing work, again. I called my husband and told him I couldn't talk about it. I'd had enough.

But then I noticed a message from a mom that read: "My daughter says today was the best day ever because she got to have Mrs. Powell ALL DAY."

I was able to show up again the following Monday, still a bit shell-shocked but ready to try again. But these experiences change us. The frustrations we face every day, from Stephen not having a pencil AGAIN to a Juul hidden on the bookcase, can wear away at us like water on stone.

And that's the force that made the Grand Canyon.

Frustration is universal, even for highly effective teachers. Like I said in my first book, *Boredom Busters*, I do believe every teacher wants to be a good teacher. But seemingly minor things irritate us, chipping away at our resolve, depleting us of the very qualities that made us fall in love with teaching in the first place.

The impact of teacher frustration is significant—we are less effective; we pass that stress on to our students, who may experience academic losses; and burnt-out teachers leave the profession at a startling (and costly) rate.

After the frustrations drip down our foreheads and onto our shoulders, day after day, do we have enough left? What's the cost? As water leeches minerals from stone, frustrations leech our creativity, patience, compassion, energy, resolve, confidence, and more. And at the end of the day, some very good teachers close the doors on their classrooms for the last time, leaving the profession entirely. Others stay, growing more bitter each day, eventually doing more harm than good to the very students they entered this profession to serve. The rest of us? We're left wondering if we have what it takes. We find ourselves feeling broken and faulty. And we've got to do it all again tomorrow.

This book isn't about telling educators what they should and shouldn't care about. Instead, I want to help you unpack your frustrations and empower you with effective ways to respond. First, in part 1, we'll look more closely at the impact of teacher frustration before moving on to what we can do about it. In part 2, a frustration flowchart and functional frustration assessment, which acknowledge and respect the fact that an issue might be minor to one reader but major to another, will help facilitate customized solutions to your frustrating experiences. Finally, in part 3, you'll find an in-depth look at a few ideas for practical application that support a positive classroom experience, to help bust frustration before it even begins.

Part 1

FRUSTRATION IS MORE THAN A FEELING

We stood outside the cafeteria in a loose clump, arms crossed, eyes downcast. After ushering our students to an assembly during their fifth-period specials time, we lingered. Although we all had mountains of work to get to, not one of us was in a hurry to get back to our rooms. Finally, one of my colleagues said, "I just feel like I'm failing today."

"Oh, thank God!" another said.

You can imagine us all turning our heads to blink at her.

"What?" she replied. "I thought it was just me!"

Every single one of us was a veteran teacher. Every one of us was rated effective or highly effective by our administrators. Every one of us was a creative and dedicated professional. And every single one of us was feeling defeated.

By what?

That's the thing—we hadn't any idea what. It hadn't been a bad week. Nothing dramatic had happened. But there we stood, dedicated, experienced professionals, complaining about our students.

Complaining about our students.

I complained about my students.

Nearly half my first period arrived to class with dead Chromebooks. It's a small thing, but we use those Chromebooks *so much* all day, and I have just four outlets in my room. And, wouldn't you know it, several of those students with dead Chromebooks didn't have their chargers. So they had to interrupt other students to ask to borrow one. Some of those students had to go to their lockers to get theirs. After a few days of this, I was at my wit's end. Unfortunately, instead of complaining about the problem, naming my frustration, or seeking solutions, I complained about my kids.

I wasn't the only one. From students not completing work and appearing apathetic to being chronically tardy to class, we all had *something*, like a pebble in our shoe, that had worn us down that week.

That moment has stuck with me. It was in that moment that I realized just how significant these individually insignificant frustrations are. These minor irritations broke a team of expert teachers! And that definitely affected our students.

That's why this matters.

Chapter 1

The Real Cost of Teacher Frustration

If you've lived a day anything like my day of Juuls and subsequent respite on the hallway floor, you already know the impact of frustration. But if by some miracle you've been unscathed by frustration, or you're not in education and doubt the importance of our feelings, let's look at some evidence together.

According to a 2015 Center on Education Policy survey of teachers, 60 percent of respondents indicated that they're less enthusiastic about their job than when they started, and almost half said they would leave the profession if they found a higher-paying job.[1] These sentiments are echoed in other similar surveys and studies. Although the exact figure varies a bit year to year, recent data suggest that upward of 15 percent of teachers leave the profession each year and 58 percent selected the phrase "not good" to describe their mental health in a 2017 American Federation of Teachers survey.[2] Contributing factors like large class sizes, the weight of standardized testing, feeling unvalued by administration or educational policy makers, paperwork, unrealistic expectations, and even being bullied at work are often listed as reasons so many teachers have such negative outlooks on their jobs. While the reasons are myriad and complex, too much so to be distilled to one cause, the word often used to encompass the result is "burnout."

The cost of this burnout and the resulting high teacher turnover in US public schools is estimated at 7.3 billion dollars a year! Yet the cost of this turnover and stress is far more than just financial. Studies indicate that students in schools with high teacher turnover score lower in English and math.[3] In Gallup's 2014 State of American Schools report, 45 percent of students reported feeling disengaged at school, a number that trends upward by grade level.[4] On the other hand, students who reported having even just one teacher who made them feel excited were thirty times more likely to be engaged. Thirty times!

There's also evidence to suggest that teachers' stress can be passed on to their students. University of British Columbia researchers found that students had higher levels of cortisol in the morning if their teachers reported high levels of burnout.[5] We can surmise from this that having a stressed-out teacher stresses kids out. Teachers reporting higher levels of stress also employed fewer effective teaching strategies, an interesting connection between teacher stress and efficacy.[6] Another study indicated a correlation among teacher stress level, classroom management skills, and more disruptive behavior from students. Teachers who showed higher stress early in the school year displayed less effective classroom management and instruction strategies, which also affected their classroom climates.

So why are teachers so stressed out? Factors we've mentioned, such as class size, standardized testing, and even the perceived demands of meeting the diverse needs of their students, are all things beyond teachers' control. Loss of control is terrifying, and perhaps especially for teachers! We have an audience of individual, opinionated human beings under our care at any given time, many of whom are gifted at finding the chinks in our armor. That's already tough. So when something threatens our control, when something leaves us feeling even a little powerless, that's a scary feeling. To dramatically oversimplify what happens in our brains when we feel frustration, the brain perceives threat and we enter the fight-or-flight response. This is not the brain state that makes rational decisions. So rather than thoughtfully responding to frustrating classroom interruptions, we react out of raw emotion. This is why frustration can lead to poor classroom management and statistically relevant academic losses.

The pressure is always on in education. Yes, there are plenty of high-impact factors that *are* within teacher control. But think of water on stone. Even a couple stressful encounters in a day can drip, drip, drip away at a teacher's confidence, patience, and ability. And if stressed teachers lead to poor classroom management, academic losses, and stressed students, we need to be doing more to support those teachers' mental and emotional well-being.

Why is frustration so powerful? Clinical psychologist Andrea Bonior says, "Frustration is likely to be the top layer of a feeling. It speaks to a sense of stagnation or helplessness, an inability to make things happen in the way that someone wants."[7] When we expect one thing but find it didn't turn out the way we thought it would, we get frustrated.

When Frustration Masks Other Feelings

Rather than a feeling itself, frustration may actually be a symptom of some other emotional response. Bonior also says that if you feel like someone or something thwarted you, what you're perceiving as frustration may actually be anger. On my epic Juul fiasco day, I had planned an immersive escape room experience to deepen our understanding of the day's text. It was going to be *awesome*. It took so much time to create and prepare, testing every link and puzzle, carefully timing each challenge, making sure everything was organized and ready to go. When it was derailed by all the crying students, administrators coming in and out, and friends ratting friends out, I kid you not, it felt like a personal attack. It felt like they took that perfect lesson away from me. Now, I *know* that's not true. Even in the moment, I really did know that. But that's how it felt. And the worst part was that I took it personally. I believed I had a better relationship with those students than that, that they wouldn't hide a Juul in *my* room! They respected me too much for that! Ha, well, respect or not, they *did* hide a Juul in my room. They thwarted me. They made me mad.

Feeling frustrated about unknown outcomes, on the other hand, is likely really anxiety or fear. This is that loss-of-control premise. We fear what would happen if our control over our students were threatened. That's why we don't like it when a student challenges our authority. Follow that scenario a bit further, we worry, and you'll find total anarchy. It's hard to love and enjoy our students if we feel threatened by them. That fear can lead us to lock down ourselves—how we discipline, how we teach—leaving us cold and rigid, all in the name of maintaining and enforcing control. Y'all, let's be real. When my fiasco was unfolding, I had my normal class of twenty-eight students plus eight students from my colleague's class. I was trying to teach my class, catch up students who were returning late from testing, and supervise the independent work of my colleague's students. I was stressed. The room was a powder keg. I was sure any small step out of line would ignite it. Was I making sound instructional decisions? *No!* Y'all, I felt like I was in one of those gritty survivalist movies, like I was going to have to fend off a bear with nothing but my fingernails and tenacity, turn his hide into shelter, and fashion a spear out of his femur. I wasn't teaching. I was just surviving.

Hopelessness may also really be sadness masked as frustration. When we encounter these frustration scenarios again and again, day after day, and feel ineffective in our response, we wind up feeling hopeless. It's hard to love our job when we feel hopeless! We know what happens in our classroom is our responsibility, but we also feel like so many variables are out of our control. If we feel responsible for the problem, we might actually be feeling guilty. We feel guilty for not being able to successfully navigate all these problems and for the resulting impact on our students. Even though I didn't hide the Juul,

I felt responsible for it. I felt like I should have known what was happening, even though I really was barely keeping my head above water with all the other variables in play. I felt like a failure. And the resulting low self-esteem might be shame instead of frustration. We tell ourselves that if we were a good teacher, we wouldn't feel this way. We believe that the "good" teachers down the hall don't have these kinds of problems. But in reality, all of us are struggling, in our own ways. This profession is hard! When we are honest with each other about what we're struggling with, we open ourselves up to receive support.

The Importance of Support

When my colleagues gathered around me as I lay on the hall carpet, they commiserated and then laughed with me as we realized the absolute absurdity of what had just happened. They joined me in the Doritos—well, not literally *in* the Doritos . . . even their love has limits—and made sure I wasn't alone. They reminded me of the light. They helped me hang on to hope. They helped me keep that traumatic day in perspective. Hope is the antidote to frustration.

But what if I didn't have a good relationship with my coworkers and had to work through that trauma all by myself? I wouldn't have had their support, their understanding and sympathy, their ideas and suggestions. I wouldn't have been able to draw strength from them. It's hard to find your way out of the darkness without people to remind you about the light. Or sometimes the people around you are so deep in the darkness themselves that they don't remember the light. This is the dangerous side of coworker relationships. Worse perhaps than having gone through that day alone would have been if, as my coworkers gathered around me, they fed the darkness in my mind. What if they had told me kids these days are just so awful, parents are trash for not being more aware, that our administration is doing nothing about these problems, why even bother planning cool activities anyway? Drip, drip, drip. More of me would be gone, conversation by conversation, day by day, till my own job satisfaction and skill were but a faint shadow of what they formerly had been.

Like I said, during that calamity, I definitely wasn't teaching. I was simply surviving. I wasn't aware of students' needs; there was no responsive teaching, no data-driven decision-making. If I were to have been evaluated in that moment, instead of presenting as the highly effective teacher I am, I would have been found in need of improvement.

I remember when a district I worked for started looking at alternative measures to reduce the frequency of disciplinary suspensions. One new expectation was that teachers not send students to the hallway for minor classroom disruptions. As I listened to my coworkers, I heard suspicion and fear. If they couldn't boot a kid when he or she disrupted class, what would they do? Wouldn't the students see that they weren't going to be disciplined for acting out and just run amok? We took away teachers' power and didn't empower them with any other strategies. They felt threatened. Scared. Powerless. Like the surveys referenced earlier say, the majority of teachers already feel like their administrators and policy makers don't listen to them. So when they feel threatened, scared, and powerless, they are left hopeless.

That's something I've been rolling around in my head and heart ever since. If you've read *Boredom Busters*, you know empowering teachers is really important to me. You know I also believe in respecting teachers as individuals with diverse, equally valid teaching styles. There's not one right way to be a good teacher. A missing pencil might be no big deal to one teacher and a huge frustration to another. And that's OK! I mean, are we really going to say there's one right way to handle pencils? *That's* the hill we want to die on? Psh, not me. So instead of prescribing a "right" way to respond to specific frustrations, my goal is to create a process teachers can use to unpack each frustration and respond in healthy, effective ways that respect their own teaching style and goals. I want teachers to have a voice. I want teachers to be more empowered. If teachers feel more empowered, their job satisfaction and mental health will improve, freeing them up to be more effective instructors, to the benefit of all our students.

Chapter 2

I'd Explain It to You, but I Was a Ballerina

The best offense is a good defense.

Or something like that.

To be honest, my experience with offense and defense is pretty limited. I was a ballerina, and we don't have offense and defense in ballet. We have tour jetés and pas de deux. As for sports, I ran cross country. No offense or defense in that either, unless you consider trying not to run into trees a defense or outpacing the person in front of you in the chute an offense. Maybe.

In any case, my point is this: when it comes to addressing our frustration as teachers, the best offense is a good defense. Having strong relationships with our students and honoring who they are as human beings can actually prevent some of the very behaviors and issues that frustrate us most. Of course, this isn't a magic spell. There are no guarantees of satisfaction. This isn't an equation that will yield the same results every single time. But in general, when we talk about classroom management, the most effective place to start is paying attention to how we behave toward our students.

Now, wait, don't give up on me. I'm not saying that teachers who plan engaging lessons and honor students' autonomy never get frustrated. That's ridiculous. Anyone who claims being a great teacher means you're never frustrated is lying and doing a great disservice to all of us who give our very best every day but sometimes wind up lying on the floor with the Doritos.

Right?

But it is true that we can create positive conditions conducive to both student and teacher success. It's not magic. It won't prevent all frustration. But it's the right place to start when we consider improving our own efficacy and job satisfaction.

Building Strong Student-Teacher Relationships

A strong, positive relationship between the teacher and students is remarkably powerful. Like we read in chapter 1, a stressed teacher leads to stressed students, but an excited teacher leads to excited students. A relationship of trust and safety promotes deeper thinking and more engaged learning. When students feel safe with their teacher and classmates, they are more willing to take the risks necessary to make academic gains. In fact, an analysis of forty-six studies shows that relationships had a positive impact on everything from grades to attendance and discipline. The *Journal of Educational Psychology* published a study that showed the more teachers praised students, the more students were on task.[1] And off-task behavior tends to be a considerable source of teacher stress! The 2014 North Carolina Teacher of the Year, James Ford, put it this way: "Our first job as teachers is to make sure that we learn our students . . . showing respect for their culture and affirming their worthiness to receive the best education possible."

Empowering Students through Voice and Choice

A strong student-teacher relationship extends into *how* we teach our students. Students benefit from curriculum that is both challenging and achievable. That balance, what one of my professors described as "controlled floundering," means meeting students where they are and coming alongside them as they work hard to reach what's next. But how can we keep students motivated to stick with work when it's hard, especially when it's not particularly interesting for them? We can engage students in challenging work when we foster autonomy, voice, and choice. If we give students an opportunity to shape the way our classrooms run, offer choices in what work to complete or how to complete it, and support them in a way that fosters their independence, students feel empowered and respected. And—you guessed it—that minimizes yet another common area of teacher stress.

As students participate in this challenging curriculum, they make progress with specific, constructive feedback. The education researcher and author John Hattie has written a great deal about the value of feedback.[2] He says, "The key question is, does feedback help someone understand what they don't know, what they do know, and where they go? That's when and why feedback is so powerful, but a lot of feedback doesn't—and doesn't have any effect." Although feedback seems like more of a recent buzzword, Ellis Page, an education professor and researcher regarded as the father of automated essay scoring, conducted a study in 1958 examining the relationship between feedback and grades on academic growth.[3] His study showed that students who received descriptive feedback without a grade showed the most growth. This kind of feedback communicated both the teachers' high expectations and willingness to partner with the students in their success, and that they were on their side, not against them. Again, the power of relationships.

But one of the most common teacher complaints is that students just aren't motivated to do the work, especially when it's hard. Well, guess what? Relationship helps that as well! In an Association for Supervision and Curriculum Development article, the educational leadership contributor Heather Voke summarizes, "Students are motivated to learn when they believe that their teachers care about their education and about them personally."[4] Often, in an effort to motivate students to work harder or behave better, we offer extrinsic rewards.

Though extrinsic rewards are seemingly effective in the short term, the biggest impact comes when students are intrinsically motivated. Convincing a student to care about his or her academic progress can be challenging. We'll explore more about fostering intrinsic motivation in reluctant students in part 3, including my own take on gamification.

One of my favorite ways to motivate students to participate in our curriculum is to leverage novelty and fun. In my first book, *Boredom Busters*, I offer dozens of easy ways for teachers to turn worksheets, lectures, and grading into exciting, unexpected learning opportunities.[5] I'll offer a sneak peek of some of these activities later on in chapter 10. For now, suffice it to say that students are far less likely to act out and be disruptive when they're busy having fun learning.

Even teachers with strong relationships with their students sometimes find themselves frustrated when their students behave like, well, children. I remember a time our whole junior and senior high school complex had to be evacuated to the football field when a fire sensor indicated a problem. The junior high students sat on the home team side, and the high school students faced us on the visiting team side. As we stood in the sunshine and heat to supervise our students, who were bouncing around on the bleachers like popcorn in a skillet, one of my colleagues elbowed me and said, "Look at them. All they have to do is sit here. Look at the high school kids—they're sitting still. Why can't our kids do that?" Although *many* factors likely contributed to her frustration in that moment (like the unexpected interruption, loss of instructional time, no clear word on when we could go back in, the heat and subsequent sweat), what she voiced in that moment was frustration from having expectations her students simply couldn't meet. It wasn't developmentally appropriate. Whatever age you teach, you have a responsibility to make yourself well versed in the nature and development of that age. So often, we forget what it's like to be six, twelve, eighteen. And we find ourselves frustrated with our students for behaviors that are actually well explained by their developmental stage. We cannot continue to view as willful misbehavior that which may truly be development. And, if you teach adolescents like I do, may I recommend the books *The Power of the Adolescent Brain*, a quick and informative read by Thomas Armstrong, and *The Successful Middle School: This We Believe*, the Association for Middle Level Education's landmark position paper on young adolescent development and middle grades best practices.

Fostering Relationships with Families

As we consider the defensive maneuvers we can engage to prevent our own frustration, we also need to consider the importance of positive relationships with our students' parents and families. From overindulgent parents who can't believe their darling child could ever do wrong to absentee parents we just can't seem to get ahold of, families can be our strongest partners or our biggest adversaries. It's easy to lose sight of the fact that we have the same goal—we want what's best for these kids. In fact, positive parent/teacher relationships lead to some of the same benefits as positive teacher/student relationships: students do better academically, socially, and emotionally. The Early Learning Network recommends the three Cs—communication, consistency, and collaboration—to foster strong relationships with parents.[6]

Combating Professional Frustrations

Now that we've got the students and parents on our side, what about our role as a professional among our colleagues? As we examined the sources and impact of teacher stress, one of the primary factors teachers expressed again and again was feeling like administrators and policy makers don't honor teachers' voices. The high turnover rate in our field shows just how important this is. It should come as no surprise that if having a voice leads to greater achievement for our students, having a voice would also lead to greater achievement as a teacher. Just like strong student-teacher relationships are evident in classrooms in which students are empowered with authentic opportunities to shape their learning experiences, strong professional relationships are the foundation of teacher voice. Teachers benefit from feeling valued and respected by their colleagues and their administrators. However, as standards have grown more and more rigorous and standardized testing carries more and more weight, some schools have standardized just about every aspect of teachers' jobs, including what they teach, when they teach it, and even how they teach it. This rigidity and lack of respect for teachers as professionals may be a sizable contributing factor to teacher burnout and turnover. When teachers have a voice, though, they are able to use their skills and talents to meet their students' needs and shape the policies of their schools. If feeling powerless and voiceless is behind so much of our professional frustration, having a voice in the direction of our schools can prevent much of that frustration.

This is certainly not an exhaustive list of every positive practice that prevents or minimizes frustration in the teaching field. And entire books have been written on each of these concepts, so we are just scratching the surface. However, these basic tenets lay a groundwork for a healthy professional experience. For the frustrations that still manage to manifest, like weeds forcing their way between stones, we will need to examine the nature of each frustration further.

Chapter 3

The Frustration-Busting Process

Functional Frustration Assessment

When I worked as a special education teacher, I fell in love with the FBA. Functional behavior assessments are designed to help educators and team members unpack and understand student behavior. Like the frustrations we've talked about already, student misbehavior can leave us feeling powerless, disheartened, and exhausted. FBAs demystify behavior. They help us understand not just *what* the behavior is, but *why*. Once we understand the *why* (the function of the behavior), we can do something about it. This is far more effective (and positive) than just disciplining the behavior itself, which is likely to continue or escalate until the underlying need is understood and met.

I propose something similar, but for teacher frustrations. A functional frustration assessment (FFA), if you will. I think if we identify what we feel when something frustrates us and unpack *why*, we'll be better able to respond, and hopefully we'll be able to address the underlying issues more proactively. Assuming we're already conscientiously working to engage our students, promote autonomy, apply educational neuroscience, and develop motivation, this tool would be useful for addressing the frustrations that still arise. My thought is that you wouldn't use this tool for *everything* that frustrates you but rather when you've found yourself drained, discouraged, or mad over an issue that has recurred without improvement or resolution. Or the on-the-floor-with-the-Doritos moments.

If you access the digital version of this form, you can make a copy for yourself and customize it as you see fit. I based my phrasing on the research into teacher frustration and burnout referenced in chapter 2 and my own experiences and observations. Now, let me be clear—no teacher needs even more paperwork! In fact, paperwork was cited in my survey as one of the things that frustrates teachers! So please, if this seems too daunting, dogear this page, or print a copy from the website and tape it to the inside cover of your lesson plan book or next to where you keep your favorite Flair pens. Use it to help you find the light when you feel discouraged at the end of a long day. And listen to your coworkers. When you find a colleague on the floor among the Doritos crumbs, literally or metaphorically, perhaps you can say, "Hey, I read about this tool designed to help teachers unpack their frustration. Let's take a look together."

FUNCTIONAL FRUSTRATION ASSESSMENT

Describe the frustration:

This made me feel: (select all that apply)

- ☐ like I was losing control of the student(s)
- ☐ like I have no control over this issue
- ☐ like my authority was being challenged
- ☐ like my students don't like me
- ☐ like I had no say or voice
- ☐ like I was a bad teacher

- ☐ like I was losing instructional time
- ☐ like this is never going to get better
- ☐ angry
- ☐ embarrassed
- ☐ alone
- ☐ afraid
- ☐ sad
- ☐ other _____

This occurred:

- ☐ during transition into/out of class
- ☐ during transition between lesson elements
- ☐ while I lectured/talked to the whole class
- ☐ during independent work
- ☐ during partner/group work

- ☐ during rotations/ center activities
- ☐ with student technology
- ☐ with basic supplies
- ☐ when the student was with a peer or adversary
- ☐ when I was busy with something else
- ☐ other _____

*Note the day of the week, time of day, and other factors as well.

This is something I feel the student(s) involved should have known how to do/handle:

☐ Yes   ☐ No

What have I tried to do about it?

What was the result?

*Follow up with the Frustration Flowchart.

23

The same way an FBA is designed to help us understand what is behind student behavior, this functional frustration assessment is designed to help us understand how we feel about whatever frustrated us and draw sound conclusions. But it doesn't tell us what to do about it. After completing an FBA, we would create a behavior intervention plan (BIP). This is what we do about the behavior. Similarly, we'll follow up the FFA with the frustration flowchart.

I like flowcharts. All I have to do is answer some questions, and the chart will tell me what to do. I wish there was one for picking a place to eat after church. The frustration flowchart is designed to help us evaluate frustration and respond effectively. Now, again, I feel the need to be clear about a couple things. First, it would not be appropriate to pull out your flowchart to respond to every frustration you encounter in a school day. When Jillian turns around to talk to Marco for the 4,697th time this class period, you would *not* say, "Hang on, Jillian, let me see what the flowchart says to do about this. Class, sit silently at your seats while I figure this out." Nope. Instead, you can familiarize yourself with the prioritizing questions in the flowchart to help you quickly make effective decisions, even when frustrated. Or you can sit down with the flow chart after a particularly frustrating experience to make a plan how you'll respond in the future. If you've tried a couple of ideas to remedy a particular frustration but find yourself facing it again and again, this may help. Maybe when your team meets to share data and plan together, you can use this tool to address common frustrations you're seeing. If you're a coach or principal supporting teachers or a mentor guiding a new teacher, you could go through this tool together. It's a resource intended to help teachers regain power over the things that frustrate them.

Second, this flowchart is *not* for behaviors that jeopardize anyone's safety. Matters of student safety *must* be addressed *immediately*, no matter what. This flowchart is not a how-to-address-every-problematic-behavior-ever tool. Instead, it's designed to help us respond to the more *minor irritants* that arise during the school day or during our careers. For more specific examples of frustrations worked out in detail, see part 2 of this book.

And please remember, real life is complex and can't be boiled down to a series of simple questions and answers. Thus, this flowchart is imperfect. It will not lead you to the perfect solution to every problem 100 percent of the time. If I were able to create a chart that did that, I'd be both smarter and richer than I am. In short, this is a tool, and as such, it will sometimes misfire. But I hope it helps you regain power over your frustration at least some of the time.

A digital version of the flowchart is available on my website. I encourage you to dogear this page or print a copy from the site and keep it in a handy place for quick reference. In part 2 of this book, we'll use the flowchart to examine many common frustrations teachers face. You'll find specific examples and sample solutions there.

FRUSTRATION FLOWCHART

ANYTHING THAT JEOPARDIZES STUDENT SAFETY MUST BE ADDRESSED IMMEDIATELY.

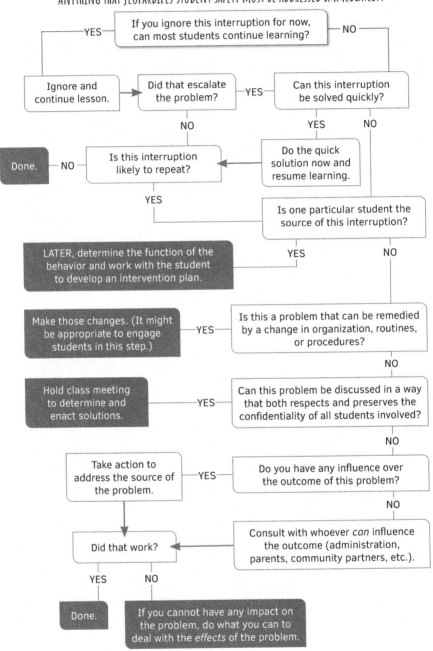

YES — If you ignore this interruption for now, can most students continue learning? — NO

Ignore and continue lesson.

Did that escalate the problem? — YES — Can this interruption be solved quickly?

NO

YES   NO

Done. — NO — Is this interruption likely to repeat?

Do the quick solution now and resume learning.

YES

Is one particular student the source of this interruption?

LATER, determine the function of the behavior and work with the student to develop an intervention plan.

YES   NO

Make those changes. (It might be appropriate to engage students in this step.) — YES — Is this a problem that can be remedied by a change in organization, routines, or procedures?

NO

Hold class meeting to determine and enact solutions. — YES — Can this problem be discussed in a way that both respects and preserves the confidentiality of all students involved?

NO

Take action to address the source of the problem. — YES — Do you have any influence over the outcome of this problem?

NO

Did that work? — Consult with whoever *can* influence the outcome (administration, parents, community partners, etc.).

YES   NO

Done.   If you cannot have any impact on the problem, do what you can to deal with the *effects* of the problem.

Part 2

Applying the FFA and Frustration Flowchart

What you'll find in the second part of the book is a sampling of this "frustration-busting" process in action. Through the highly scientific process of asking my teacher friends on Facebook and Twitter, these were identified as some of the common frustrations teachers face. My own experience concurs. In this section, we'll apply the functional frustration assessment and the frustration flowchart to each frustration, one at a time. We'll interpret each multiple ways. Whether a student showing up without a pencil feels like a minor disruption or a symptom of systemic apathy, you'll find a variation to suit your interpretation. For each, we'll explore possible solutions.

I've organized the sample frustrations loosely as classroom management frustrations, instructional frustrations, and professional frustrations. Of course there's overlap between these, but for the sake of organization, we'll pretend it's as straightforward as this.

First, classroom management frustrations.

Chapter 4

Busting Classroom Management Frustrations: Materials and Routines

Let's imagine you planned your lesson to fill each moment, bell to bell. As you transitioned from direct instruction to guided practice, you gave the directions aloud and had them projected, in writing, on your screen. Afterward, you had a handful of students repeat them back to you, verifying that you were understood. You planned which students to meet with in a small group while the rest of the class got started, then called those students over and tapped the stack of papers on your table to straighten them out as they made their way over to you. This is a normal day. No hidden Juuls. No pee-ness slips of the tongue. You look up and scan the heads bent over their work and realize Chester is picking at a spot on his arm. "Chester," you call. "Why aren't you working?"

"I don't have a pencil."

In this chapter, we'll unpack scenarios like Chester's lack of a pencil, missing laptop chargers, errant homework assignments, and other similar frustrations around materials and basic daily routines.

To some of us, no big deal. To others, *big deal*. See, that's the thing. Even if the causes of our frustrations are pretty universal, the way they make us feel is anything but. I'm not writing this book to tell you what you should do when something like this happens to you. I don't think there *is* one right thing to do! Instead, we can unpack these kinds of scenarios bit by bit and explore a variety of different ways to respond. Hopefully you'll find a response among them that honors your own feelings and goals. Note that we'll continue to discuss missing materials in the sections that follow using the example of Chester and his absent pencil, but remember that this could stand in for any number of supplies students may forget to bring to class.

Let's look at the frustration flowchart together. Consider the first question: "If you ignore this interruption for now, can most students continue learning?" If we ignore Chester for now, what will happen? Hopefully, he'll quietly ask around to borrow a pencil. Or perhaps you already have a system in place for dealing with a missing pencil (or paper or charger) that he should be familiar with so he can borrow that item himself. In either case, most students are working and ignoring this situation does not escalate the problem, so we would answer "yes" to the first and second questions. You also know that Chester typically comes to class prepared, so this issue is unlikely to repeat.

The Chronically Underprepared Student

But what if turns out you need to fix an underlying problem? Maybe Chester just forgot today, or his pencil rolled off his desk and disappeared. But what if he doesn't have a pencil again tomorrow? And he didn't have one yesterday? Well, in that case, though ignoring his missing pencil now didn't escalate the problem and Chester was able to find a pencil to get by, we're going to find ourselves dealing with this same problem later. In which case, yes, this problem is likely to repeat. We can also see that, since most students were working, this is an isolated problem specifically involving our Chester.

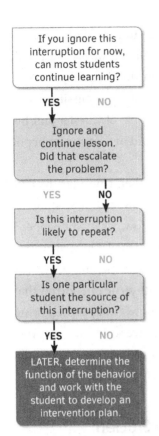

If you ignore this interruption for now, can most students continue learning?

YES — NO

Ignore and continue lesson. Did that escalate the problem?

YES — **NO**

Is this interruption likely to repeat?

YES — NO

Is one particular student the source of this interruption?

YES — NO

LATER, determine the function of the behavior and work with the student to develop an intervention plan.

When a frustration centers around one student, there are a couple of pitfalls we can easily tumble into if we aren't careful. One is that we overcorrect and make sweeping procedural changes to address something that really was already working successfully for the majority of students. If Chester didn't have a pencil but everyone else was prepared and working fine, there's likely no reason to make a brand-new pencil-borrowing system for the whole class. The second potential pitfall is to take Chester's lack of pencil personally, and instead of being frustrated at the fact Chester didn't have a pencil, we are frustrated at Chester.

Deep breath here, y'all. Remember, I live in the real world too. I'm far from perfect. I've complained about kids.

But Chester *is* a kid. He's a *kid*. Just as any human—myself included—is far from perfect, Chester is a still-developing person, by his very nature not done learning how to be one yet. He didn't choose to be a child. And education is compulsory in the United States, so he probably didn't even choose to be a student, let alone a student in our class. Sure, he may have chosen to come without a pencil. He may not have. But either way, we chose to be teachers. So, in this moment, we're allowed to be frustrated. But we have to guard ourselves against projecting that frustration onto Chester.

That's where the functional frustration assessment helps. If I fill out the FFA the way this pencil scenario makes *me* feel, it looks like this:

This made me feel:
☑ like I was losing instructional time
☑ like this is never going to get better
This occurred:
☑ during transition between lesson elements
☑ during independent work
☑ with basic supplies
☑ when I was busy with something else
This is something I feel the student(s) involved should have known how to do/handle:
☑ Yes

I can start to see that I get frustrated at the loss of instructional time—the flow of my lesson—and that I expect all the students, Chester included, to know how to come to class prepared and meet such basic needs as this.

The flowchart suggested I meet with Chester to determine the function of his behavior—coming to class without the necessary materials. If I don't rein in my own emotions before I do that, my conversation with Chester isn't likely to go well.

Now, if I sit down with Chester, quietly after class or when other students are occupied, and I ask him about not having a pencil, it's probably going to take a while to get past, "I don't know. I don't have one."

If a particular student doesn't have the things they're required to have in class, and it seems to be a chronic problem for them, perhaps consider:

- Does the student *have* the supplies they need? If not, would his parents be able to buy them if you let them know he's been without? Maybe Chester just never told them he was out. If not, can you quietly provide him with some? It's likely your school has some supplies set aside for needs like this. Supplies like pencils aren't terribly expensive if you wind up trying to bridge this gap on your own. Area businesses, sports teams, tourist sites, and other sources probably even have branded pencils they'd give you! More expensive materials may require other solutions. Even if you have the world's best parent-teacher organization standing by to donate to your classroom whenever you ask, I doubt you have a bulk supply of laptop chargers. For items like these, we can start by trying to track down what's missing. Again, the student may not have told his or her parents that the item's missing. It may be easy to locate at home with a little family assistance. It may be sitting in a lost and found. It may be in another student's bag. However, if it's truly gone, we can engage in our school's process for how the family can request a replacement.

- Does this student have the necessary supplies but isn't bringing them? Perhaps he's avoiding the work. Does it feel too hard? Is he dealing with emotions that preclude his ability to attend to his work? Perhaps Chester has a classmate he'd like to be partnered with, or he could be seated nearer to you, join your small group, or do a few problems with you until he's able to continue on his own.

- Is Chester struggling with organization? Maybe when he's at his locker, he's grabbing his textbooks and folders but not his pencils. Maybe he doesn't use a pencil case of any kind, so the pencils keep rolling away or dropping when he's walking down the hall. As the educators and adults in our students' world, we often mistakenly assume our students naturally understand how to be organized. Sometimes they don't. We can support Chester by posting a list of needed daily materials in his locker and teaching him to check the list before shutting the locker and heading to class. Maybe we show him a few organizational tools like various kinds of pencil cases and binders and let him pick the tools that make the most sense to him. We can even check in with Chester when we greet him at the door each day and prompt him to check through his supplies to make sure he's ready before he heads to his desk.

- It's likely that something as small as any of the frustrations we're dealing with in this book doesn't need a formal if/then plan or behavior contract. Again, we're focusing on minor irritants, not major behaviors of concern. If Chester's lack of organization and preparation is actually a sign of a more significant issue or need, like an underlying disability or trauma at home, Chester is going to benefit from far more than a plan that addresses his missing pencil. We need to engage in our school's appropriate intervention process, including expanding our response to include counselors, interventionalists, special education teachers, or other related service providers. In any case, if Chester seems to need goals or rewards to work toward, in your professional judgment, perhaps you can set a goal that Chester come to class prepared with a pencil for a full school week and then can eat lunch in your room with two other friends (or whatever your Chester is motivated to work toward).

To borrow a summarization approach from the internet, here's the "too long; didn't read" (TL;DR): Chester didn't have a pencil, and he's not likely to have one tomorrow either. He can figure out how to get one today, but you're going to have to solve this problem again tomorrow. You meet with Chester to figure out why he doesn't bring a pencil and, together, make a plan to address that problem.

The Escalator

Let's backtrack and imagine, though, that when I initially ignore Chester's missing pencil, instead of quickly finding one and getting to work, he just continues to sit there, picking at the spot on his arm. Or his solution for not having a pencil is to stand up and yell, "Anyone got a pencil?" Or to go up and down each row like the cotton candy guy at a Pacers game?

Now ignoring the problem has escalated it. What shall we do?

After the escalation, we look for the quick solution. The goal *isn't* to make an example of Chester in the middle of class. The goal is to preserve learning. So we quietly grab a pencil for Chester and get him started. Then you can see that the flowchart takes us right back where we were before: later, we work with Chester one-on-one to solve the problem together.

If you ignore this interruption for now, can most students continue learning?

YES   NO

Ignore and continue lesson. Did that escalate the problem?

YES   NO

Can this interruption be solved quickly?

YES   NO

Do the quick solution now and resume learning. Is this interruption likely to repeat?

YES   NO

Is one particular student the source of this interruption?

YES   NO

LATER, determine the function of the behavior and work with the student to develop an intervention plan.

TL;DR: If ignoring the missing pencil escalates the problem, quickly provide a pencil to preserve learning, then later work with the student to arrange a long-term solution.

Learning Interference

This interpretation backs all the way up to Chester's original missing pencil. Let's say, this time, we believe the fact that Chester cannot work without his pencil means this problem actually *does* get in the way of his ability to continue to learn. In this case, we go down the "no" side of the chart.

From there, we see that we'll still offer whatever quick solution allows us to keep our focus on the learning for now. The missing pencil is likely to repeat (it is, after all, one of the most common complaints teachers raised in my super unscientific inquiry online). From there, we either address it individually with Chester or class-wide via a procedural change, whichever best addresses our specific situation.

This kind of scenario can occur with any number of materials, and if your school uses student devices, it can be infuriating. If you've taken the time to plan an engaging lesson using effective tech tools, it can be more than a little frustrating when students come to class with dead Chromebooks and no charger and aren't prepared to participate. And the more interactive and immersive tech tools get, the less likely it is that you can prepare for uncharged devices by simply providing some paper copies. Some tech tools just can't be replicated on paper.

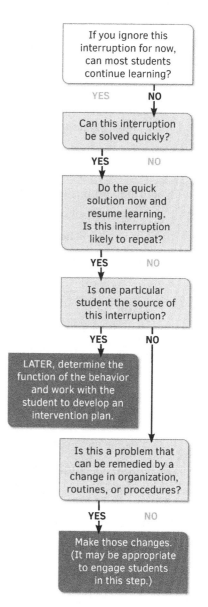

Like with a missing pencil, an uncharged device might be a problem with one student, meaning other students are able to keep learning. If you ignore the issue and the devices are part of a normal enough routine in your classroom, they might be able to figure it out. They may be able to ask around, find a charger to borrow, and plug in to one of the outlets available in the room.

But what if instead of an uncharged device, our student—let's call her Macy—has lost her charger. It's been gone for about two weeks already. It's unlikely that Chromebook's going to magically be charged tomorrow. Although the problem did not escalate, it is likely to repeat.

In meeting with Macy one-on-one, we decide to send information about purchasing a new charger to her parents, who were financially able to afford replacement. In the meantime, our plan was that Macy would be responsible for taking her Chromebook to the tech office before she left school each day to charge there overnight (barring a need to use it for homework, in which case she would plug it in when she arrived at school in the morning).

TL;DR: If not having something like a pencil, device charger, or worksheet prohibits learning, address it quickly, and then follow up with the student or a class-wide procedural change as appropriate. A dead Chromebook can be plugged in, but a missing charger's going to require a more permanent solution.

A Missing Materials Epidemic

Ah, but we're not done with pencils yet. See how a seemingly simple problem can actually be quite complex?

Let's rewind back to Chester's missing pencil. This time, we ignore it and it doesn't escalate the problem, but it's still likely to repeat. But when we consider the potential for repetition, we realize it isn't just

Chester—lots of students have come to class without pencils at some point.

This time, since the problem is likely to repeat but isn't centered around a particular student, we can look at procedural solutions.

Perhaps you just keep a cup of pencils in the room that students can borrow from as they see fit. You can walk the hallways after school to rescue lost pencils for this purpose. The superstar evening custodian, Deb, at my school loved knowing she could put the errant pencils she found after school to use in my room and refilled my cup, literally and figuratively, by bringing any pencils she found to my collection. Or you can stock your pencil cup using those promotional pencils I mentioned earlier. Some teachers have students leave collateral of some kind. Just an "I live in the real world too" word of caution, though. A teacher on our team used to have students give a shoe when they borrowed a pencil.

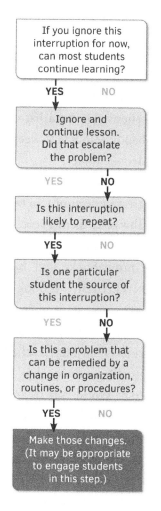

That creates an easy way to remember to give the pencil back. But one day, while she was working with other students, a couple of boys hid a girl's shoe. We literally did not find it until the end of the day. The potential for embarrassment or loss of fresh kicks Mom and Dad spent hard-earned green to provide seems worth some consideration.

If we think back to our functional frustration assessment, we may realize what bothers us about missing pencils is that we believe our students should be responsible enough to come to class prepared. One possible class-wide solution for that is to mildly reward coming to class prepared. For example, if you use ClassDojo or some other token or point system, perhaps students lay their required supplies on the corner of their desk during bell work, and you quickly scan the room and award a point to everyone who came to class prepared.

Don't forget, though, to set developmentally appropriate expectations. Maybe a list of what is required for your class would be a handy resource to keep on your classroom door or next to your students' cubbies.

When we find ourselves addressing class-wide problems, this is a great opportunity to tag in our students to help us generate solutions. This gives them a voice in how their world works and promotes buy-in.

What if instead we're dealing with an epidemic of dead Chromebooks and missing chargers and it's time for our spring NWEA test? We took our spring NWEA test the week of March 9, 2020. You remember this week. We were facing a full moon, Friday the thirteenth, and standardized testing (during which our school runs on an altered schedule—read: lunch forty-five minutes later than usual), on the cooling heels of what the students were sure was going to be World War III and the beginning of what eventually became the Events No One Wants to Ever Talk About Again (otherwise known as the COVID-19 pandemic).

Late in the week, there would be growing certainty that we would close our school for the following week in response to the beginning of the COVID-19 pandemic. Like many schools in the United States—and across the world—we did eventually announce our building's closure that Friday.

But on Tuesday the tenth, I didn't know any of that. It was just the week of a full moon and Friday the thirteenth, standardized testing, and an altered schedule. I was frazzled. I did my best to get the students into the classroom and seated so I could quickly take attendance, dismiss my students who test with accommodations in different locations, and get the test started.

But then I heard Macy say, "My Chromebook's dead."

Big sigh from me. "Well, OK, go grab your charger."

"I lost it."

Bigger sigh. "Why didn't you charge at the tech office charging station before class, then?"

"I dunno."

"Mine's dead too."

"I've got five percent."

"I think my sister has my charger."

"My charger's at my dad's. I won't see him again till spring break. I think."

Oh yeah. Long before we were concerned about passing the coronavirus to each other, it seemed we'd already spread a contagious condition of uncharged devices.

So, what do we do?

This time, we're going to do our best to get everyone a charger (which requires a panicked call to the tech office) and get them on with the assessment. Quick(ish) solution. But, again, this is likely to keep happening, especially if we keep rescuing them. Unfortunately, this can be a potential side effect of providing the quick, quiet solution that allows students to keep working. So we again need to consider procedural changes that will encourage students to be more responsible for their devices.

Like with the pencil, this could be a simple classroom reward system. Coming to class with your device charged is part of coming to class prepared, just like bringing a pencil and textbooks. Perhaps students who come to class prepared get a point. I prefer that over a consequence for the opposite. At one time, I had been deducting a point from every student with an uncharged Chromebook for weeks before a girl pulled me aside and explained that one of her classmates didn't have electricity at home. I can't hold a twelve-year-old accountable for her family's lack of electricity.

Our plan still needs to address how to proceed with students who have lost their charger, or, like this student, truly could not charge at home. For us, we decided to ask our tech team to come in to scan the barcodes on everyone's charger to make sure the charger each student had was actually the one assigned to them. Our awesome tech staff then checked the barcodes of all lost-and-found chargers against my list of students who still hadn't found their chargers. We sent parents replacement pricing info and made sure all students knew where the charging station in the tech office was so they could have a fully charged device before class, even if they couldn't find their charger or afford to replace it. Maybe not a perfect solution, but we covered as many bases as we could.

> **TL;DR:** If pencil-less-ness or charger-less-ness is sweeping your class like an epidemic, consider procedural changes that meet the underlying need and your goals for the class.

Forgotten Materials

A pencil or charger can be borrowed. But what about when a student has forgotten something that can't? What if they have to go back to their locker (or cubby) to get it, or if they left an essential item at home?

Right as my first period class began, I was stopped by Ivan and Javin.

"Look, Mrs. Powell, I have a notebook *and* pencils!" Ivan said.

Ivan had been coming to class for weeks without these basic supplies. I'm embarrassed to admit it had gone on so long before I managed a solution, but this was 2021, teaching in the pandemic world, and as many of you know, we were all doing our best to stay afloat. I should have contacted his parents to let them know he was out of supplies far earlier than I had. But once I tagged them in, he came to class fully prepared.

Almost.

"But I was so excited to grab these, I left my Chromebook at home."

Y'all, I didn't even have time to start my happy dance before he took the wind right out of my sails again. There'd be no tooting of my own horn, no chance to award myself teacher of the year. Nope.

Then Javin said, "I left my folder in my locker. Can I go get it?"

Confession time: I forget things all the time. I understand how easy it is to leave something at home in the morning rush out the door.

Mornings and I do NOT get along well. The peace treaty I've struck with mornings includes strong organization (leaving needed items in the same place every day), consistent routines, and making sure everything is ready to go before I go to bed instead of trusting myself to do it in the morning. With these strategies, I'm able to function pretty successfully.

Even still, I'm pretty sure there's some kind of time warp between fixing my hair and the moment my kids and I need to be pulling out of the driveway. I don't know where the rest of the morning goes, but it's gone before I know it. I've flown out the door without my favorite diet caffeinated beverage, my morning medication, my phone, and, yes, even without my Chromebook.

My kids have left home without their coats. And I'm a teacher mom.

So, yes, I can have mercy on my students when they confess something important has been left in their locker or at home. We are, after all, only human. We are imperfect. And I know so much of their morning is heavily dependent on how their family or household functions together.

I can easily offer mercy. But mercy doesn't miraculously retrieve Javin's folder or provide Ivan a Chromebook for today's lesson.

If I look at the functional frustration assessment, it's easy for me to see why these scenarios really burn me up. Unpacking my emotional response to these situations, I find it's essentially the same for when supplies are left in lockers as when they're left at home, although the left-it-at-home scenario can feel *more* frustrating since the item isn't easy to procure for class.

This made me feel:
   ☑ like I was losing instructional time
   ☑ like this is never going to get better

This occurred:
   ☑ during transition between lesson elements
   ☑ with basic supplies

This is something I feel the student(s) involved should have known how to do/handle.   ☑ Yes

Loss of instructional time is a *huge* pet peeve of mine. Everything I put in a lesson has a purpose. I plan for every moment. There's not *time* to find another Chromebook for Ivan or send Javin to his locker—again (not to mention, Javin would be out there unsupervised, which is far from ideal and against my school's rules). And I think I also react to that lower box, the fact that I tend to think my students *should* be able to come to class prepared. I have a list of required materials outside the door. If anything special is needed, it's posted with their bell work. I tell them in the hallway. I remind them on the way in. And yet, wouldn't you know it, not everyone shows up with what they need. Even if it's something they need every day. So here we go.

The Occasional Forgetter

Let's start at the top and imagine that whatever is missing for Javin or Ivan causes mild irritation, but today really can continue more or less undisrupted without it, and the student can bring whatever it was tomorrow. If everyone else has what they need and can focus on their learning, and this really was an isolated "oops" for this student, the problem is essentially solved. Aside from the mere human weakness of occasionally forgetting things, this scenario is not a symptom of some larger underlying problem. We can make it clear to this student what will happen if they forget it again, but chances are high the student is also feeling the irritation of having forgotten this thing and will avoid feeling this way again. The interruption to our day is too mild to disrupt parents to ask them to bring it in. We can make an extra copy of a worksheet, provide a loaner Chromebook, have the student bring their assignment in tomorrow, and move on in peace.

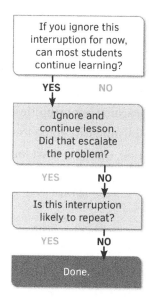

TL;DR: When the item not brought to class is minor enough not to interrupt learning today and is unlikely to repeat in the future, ignore it and move on.

The Escalator

Now let's imagine that ignoring a problem will escalate it. What if a student hasn't forgotten something mild, something minor? They've forgotten an assignment we will be building on during class, or their Chromebook on a day when this is an essential tool for learning.

In this scenario, ignoring the frustration is really not an option. Our student can't do whatever they're supposed to do without the forgotten item, and if I ignore it, they will just sit there, unable to access the lesson. That's not acceptable. Even if my policy is that if students forget to bring an assignment to class, it gets counted as missing, they're now stuck unable to participate in this part of class. (To me, even someone leaving class to go to their locker is an escalation. Perhaps it's not to you. But in my experience, this suddenly becomes the most enthralling thing to ever happen. You'd think Thor just walked in with Aquaman, made it rain starched Benjamins, and offered everyone a brand-new PlayStation.) If the point of all this is to provide the best possible learning opportunities for our students, then excluding a student from learning isn't going to work. Javin and Ivan need their supplies. In this case, our flow chart looks a bit different.

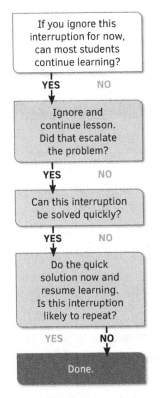

We need to move to whatever quick solution will allow our student to step back in and participate. Maybe the tech department can issue Ivan a loaner Chromebook for the day, or we can call Grandma and see if she can bring it in. Neither of these solutions is ideal but both grant Ivan access to the learning activities. We're also imagining in this version of the scenario that Ivan is *not* likely to forget his Chromebook again, that this was a one-off "oops."

This scenario also applies to things like forgotten lunches—a student *must* eat. Maybe a school meal can be provided instead of the packed lunch they've left at home or a meal provided despite lunch money left at home. If someone at home is gracious enough to do so, someone can bring the forgotten lunch into school.

> **TL;DR:** If the item forgotten is critical to learning, provide a loaner or—when appropriate—ask someone to bring it in from home.
>
> A student going back to their locker or having Grandma run in a missing project can be very disruptive. But not letting them get or have what they need could exclude them from participating in the learning.

The Chronic Forgetter

What if the problem is mostly the individual student's, but this wasn't just a one-off "oops"? Let's back up for a moment and think about Ivan's scenario. Do you see a clue that this forgotten Chromebook situation is likely to repeat? Ivan had been coming to class for an extended period of time without basic supplies. His parents *had* these supplies at home; Ivan just wasn't bringing them. Knowing that about Ivan, we may suspect this forgotten Chromebook situation will not be an isolated incident.

Whether the item is major or minor, when the problem of forgotten materials is chronic, we need to develop a more permanent plan.

We first need to be careful not to assume they really *can* meet this expectation. Anything affecting executive function—age, ADHD, learning disabilities, past trauma, and a host of other circumstances—would make the seemingly basic expectation of bringing supplies to class quite difficult. So what's our long-term solution?

After reuniting Ivan and his Chromebook, we need to sit down with him to figure out what's going on and develop a plan to help him remember his material in the future.

Let's imagine that Ivan has a known learning disability and is a bit less mature than his same-age classmates, and he definitely has deficits in executive functioning that impact his ability to be prepared and organized. Because Ivan's family was so

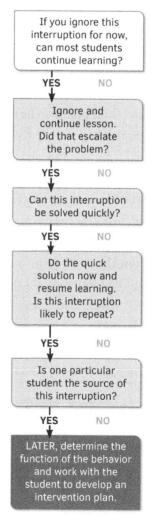

helpful when he needed supplies, we decide to tag them in. We ask for their help to remind Ivan to plug in his Chromebook each night and grab it in the morning. This will help extend organizational support into Ivan's home environment.

I fully acknowledge that's not always an option, nor is it something we have any direct control over.

Regardless of the degree of support a student does or doesn't have at home, we need to consider how to support him at school to encourage him to be organized. Maybe Ivan *loves* to pick prizes out of the treasure chest, and we already have a class point system that allows him to earn that treat. Rather than arranging individual reward plans with *each* student who struggles with these kinds of challenges, you can try to customize their class reward system experience to help them stay motivated. We can remind Ivan that coming to class prepared will earn him points so he can get a prize more often.

Perhaps we try giving Javin a list of supplies for each class to hang in his locker, and we give Ivan and his parents a list to keep at home. If there's not a list posted outside of the classroom, we post one there too. Maybe we tape a small one to the cover of their agendas or the corners of their desks and rehearse checking them when they arrive to class. Or we assign a classroom buddy to stop at his locker with him and help him check to see he has what he needs. The goal, after all, is that our students are fully able to participate in their education.

As with rescuing students from forgotten pencils or uncharged Chromebooks, quick solutions can actually feed the problem if they're not followed up with strong procedural changes.

> **TL;DR:** Make learning the priority, but then support development of the organizational skills your student needs to do better next time. When a student has challenges that affect their ability to stay organized or come prepared, a team effort is ideal.

A Forgotten Materials Epidemic

But what if it's not that one student keeps showing up without what they need, but rather, occasionally, many different students don't have what they need? It's not contagious, like the uncharged Chromebooks seemed to be, but rather isolated but annoying cases of different students coming to class without everything they need. In this case, we can't solve the problem by making individual plans with all the students. And it may not be that we need a change to our procedures or organizational systems. What if it turns out that you shore up your procedures and the problem keeps happening? What if it turns out that students really do need to step up their effort to come to class prepared?

In this case, because it's not an issue with a specific student, and because we've made sure we have strong procedures in place, we can give the students the opportunity to participate in the problem and work together to generate possible solutions. Let's imagine in our scenario that students admit they have stopped checking the supply list outside the classroom after the first few weeks of school. They acknowledge that proper support is already in place, but they need to step up and use it. Together they decide that all students who come to class unprepared should have to use notebook paper and pencil to handwrite whatever they left in their locker. This would work for a worksheet or notes, but not for a forgotten textbook. So

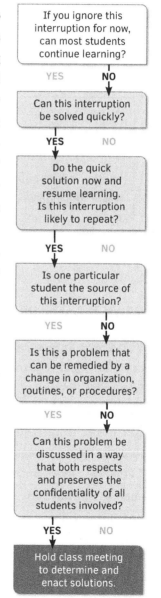

If you ignore this interruption for now, can most students continue learning?

YES   **NO**

Can this interruption be solved quickly?

YES   NO

Do the quick solution now and resume learning. Is this interruption likely to repeat?

YES   NO

Is one particular student the source of this interruption?

YES   **NO**

Is this a problem that can be remedied by a change in organization, routines, or procedures?

YES   **NO**

Can this problem be discussed in a way that both respects and preserves the confidentiality of all students involved?

YES   NO

Hold class meeting to determine and enact solutions.

you guide them to refine their plan to be something simple enough for you to enforce for any forgotten item. After reconvening, the class decides one student in each row will check that every student in their row has what they need for class, helping to locate a replacement or loaner item or sending students back to their locker quickly before the bell to retrieve anything neglected. Then, rows that are fully prepared by the bell will get a point in the class reward system, allowing rows to compete against each other and encouraging students to support each other.

> **TL;DR:** Weaknesses in our procedures and the quick solutions we use to limp along can lead to unpreparedness of epidemic proportions. It may be time to revisit procedures, make sure everyone is capable of meeting those expectations, and then follow through consistently. If strong procedures are already in place and attainable for all students, the class may be able to come up with a solution together.

What If Forgetting Is Not Just Forgetting?

Before we move on from this particular flowchart, I want to consider one additional scenario. Let's say in addition to the factors affecting Ivan's or Javin's ability to be organized and prepared, they are also disengaged or potentially avoiding participating in the work. That's a realistic possibility. If a student *does* struggle academically, it's reasonable to consider he's "forgetting" supplies as a way to avoid participating. In that case, the plan arranged with the student would need to include supports to meet his or her academic needs in a way that feels safe and sustainable.

> **TL;DR:** Sometimes "forgetting" supplies is code for "This work feels too hard" or "I don't want to do it."

Bathroom Breaks

You've just delivered a mic-drop lesson. The students are eating out of the palm of your hand. You are on cloud nine. A hand shoots up, and you eagerly call on the student, sure they're about to share some profound revelation.

"Can I go to the bathroom?"

You stammer a moment, aghast.

"That?! *That* is what you wanted to say? After the lesson we just had, *you want to go to the bathroom?*" It's hard to not take it personally, right?

This made me feel:

☑ like I have no control over this issue

☑ like I was losing instructional time

This occurred:

☑ during transition into/out of class

☑ during transition between lesson elements

☑ while I lectured/talked to the whole class

☑ during independent work

☑ during partner/group work

☑ during rotations/center activities

☑ with student technology

☑ with basic supplies

☑ when the student was with a peer or adversary

☑ when I was busy with something else

After filling in my functional frustration assessment, I can see that the loss of instructional time frustrates me, and I struggle with the fact that I really have no control over students' bodily functions. I also can't help but feel that needing to potty at what I perceive as exciting parts of class reflects poorly on my instructional planning. Maybe it doesn't really, but it's still how I feel.

I also see that needing to go to the bathroom happens any time throughout class. Yeah, sometimes kids are on a schedule. They know their best friend (or crush) will be there at that time, or I can anticipate them asking any time we switch to independent work, but for the most part, someone is asking to go to the bathroom pretty much at any time during class.

So what do we do? Your school may have procedures regarding bathroom use you're expected to follow. For various safety reasons, many schools strictly regulate and supervise bathroom use. That's understandable and supersedes other options we'll explore here. But if your situation is like mine, you find yourself in limbo between the expectation that you not send students to the bathroom at unscheduled times except for emergencies and the fact that you have no way to know for sure what constitutes an emergency when it comes to another human being's bathroom needs.

"I Need to Use the Bathroom" Epidemic

Let's start with the scenario of contagious pee-ness I referenced in my infamous hidden vape day. In this scenario, lots of students are asking to go potty at various times throughout the class time, day after day.

There are a number of ways we could interpret and analyze this scenario. For this example, I've chosen to assume most students are still learning—that even though it *feels* like everyone is asking to go potty, it's not everyone all at once, and the rest of the class is still working. I can temporarily ignore or say "We'll go in a few minutes," "Is it an emergency?" or just "No." But unless the student was bored and looking for a field trip, their bladder or bowels are not going to be satisfied with this answer. I'm going to have to make a decision. Soon.

I won't tell you what that decision should be. My own opinion tends to be that access to a bathroom respects students' humanity. I know what it feels like to go to the bathroom after lunch and wind up crossing my legs to try to make it to the bathroom again just twenty minutes later. And I'm an adult. I also know some of my students are dealing with body changes they haven't yet mastered that may leave them feeling vulnerable, embarrassed, insecure, or unclean. If I tell some students no, they can go back to their seat and wait till later. But some students will go to their seat and be totally preoccupied with their bodily need. Ever been on a road trip and someone declares that the car isn't stopping for the next hour? And suddenly you really, really have to go? It's all you can think about, isn't it? You try different postures. You try creative thinking. But your bladder starts to ache. You start to break out in a sweat. You start to do the math of mile markers and the clock with each exit you pass.

You may have many valid reasons for saying no. You may have school policies. You may plan to take the whole class down in just a few minutes. You may know this student was caught climbing the stall walls just yesterday. You may know this student was overheard arranging to meet up with her boyfriend at precisely 10:52. You may know the student doesn't like fractions and is likely avoiding his work.

You are the expert in your classroom.

Regardless of what my temporary answer is to get me through this moment, I've got to address my classroom procedures and expectations to solve this problem more effectively for the future.

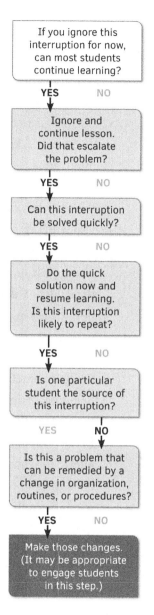

Here are some possible bathroom procedures:

- Provide scheduled, supervised class breaks and say no to visits outside of those scheduled times. (Again, note my own thoughts about this approach above.)
- Use a sign-in/sign-out system to track trips out of the room. This lets you keep an eye on who is leaving at set times, going often, gone unreasonably long, and so forth to follow up with specific issues as needed, *and* helps you keep track of who's out in the event of an emergency.
- Use a ticket system. Although not always literally a ticket, students can be given a certain number of passes out of the room each day/week/term. When those passes are used up, the student will not be allowed to leave. OK, let's be clear—I'm not suggesting you let a student risk an accident. I believe very much in respecting our students as human beings, and all human beings have some very basic needs we simply must address sometimes! The premise behind this approach is to help make trips out of the classroom more tangible and limit them to true needs.
- Limit how many students may be out at any given time, but allow students to leave as needed within those restrictions. I tried this out during COVID restrictions. Only three students could be in the bathroom at any time, so every teacher in my hall had one pass for each bathroom. If that pass was out, the next student would have to wait until it returned. I still experienced more bathroom use than I was accustomed to, but the system was fairly organized and easy to manage.
- A similar approach uses a pass or even a bottle of sanitizer a student places on their desk when they leave to access the bathroom. You can see who's out, and other students know they can't go until that student returns.

One other strategy I like has to do with *how* students ask to use the bathroom. If I'm busy with another student or vital instruction, I really don't like to be interrupted to be asked if someone can use the bathroom. Instead, I have had students stand up (so I notice them) and make a sign language "r" to signal they need to use the restroom. We practice this early in the year, and I post signage in the room. When I see them, I give them a thumbs-up if they may leave immediately or a thumbs-down if I want them to wait a moment for some reason. The student could then signal to ask again in a few minutes. I can respond to all of this without missing a beat of whatever else I am doing. Similarly, some teachers use some of the systems listed above this way—students may dismiss themselves without asking the teacher directly using the system their teacher has established.

> **TL;DR:** It's frustrating when a bathroom request derails a successful lesson, but students are human and do have basic needs. Rather than getting overwhelmed with requests, implement, practice, and stick to a system that allows class to keep moving.

The Frequent Requester

Let's imagine, though, that we've got a chronic pee-er. We've established our class-wide system, it's running smoothly, students' needs are respectfully met with minimal disruption to learning, but *someone* is visiting the bathroom far more frequently than you'd expect—and at inopportune times.

For me, this student is Kimmy. I'll talk more about Kimmy in a later scenario. Kimmy is almost always about a minute late to class. I'll see her standing at a friend's locker, then opening her own seconds before the bell rings. She'll arrive to class, late, and then ask to get her water bottle or pencil out of her locker (which she was just

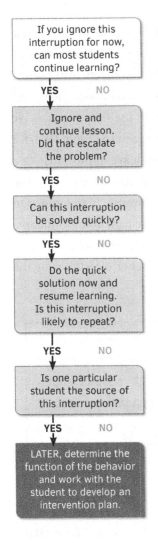

If you ignore this interruption for now, can most students continue learning?

YES — NO

Ignore and continue lesson. Did that escalate the problem?

YES — NO

Can this interruption be solved quickly?

YES — NO

Do the quick solution now and resume learning. Is this interruption likely to repeat?

YES — NO

Is one particular student the source of this interruption?

YES — NO

LATER, determine the function of the behavior and work with the student to develop an intervention plan.

at seconds before). I'll address that, we'll get class started, and then Kimmy's up, maybe ten inches from my belly, asking, "Can I go to the bathroom?" Kimmy sometimes goes twice an hour.

And Kimmy doesn't have any documented health needs.

I can either send Kimmy to the bathroom or delay her, but no matter what, she's going to ask again. And I'm going to feel frustrated, again. So I need to meet with Kimmy to find out more about what's going on. I may also need to talk to her parents or guardians just in case something else may be happening behind the scenes. But let's assume, for this example, that Kimmy does not have a medical reason to need to potty so often. When I talk with Kimmy, she expresses that she really does feel like she needs to use the bathroom that often. She explains that she gets nervous when she has to hold it. I also suspect Kimmy needs a better outlet for her scads of energy. Even though we move often in class, she might like the release of taking a quick walk, by herself, before returning to her seat. Kimmy might not have the insight to be able to communicate this to me yet, but my professional opinion is supported by the fact that, regardless of whether she needs to relieve her bladder or her sensory system, stepping out of the room for a moment is meeting her needs.

However, Kimmy is a bit behind where I'd like her to be academically. She spends a great deal of time out of her seat already (you'll hear more about that soon), and she resists working hard. I need Kimmy in class. I need her to give focused attention to her work.

So Kimmy and I arrange a compromise: Kimmy may have two passes out of the room to use each day. She can use them to visit her locker or the bathroom. Once those passes are used up each day, Kimmy cannot go again. Realistically, this doesn't leave Kimmy at any significant risk or discomfort because she has built-in passing periods positioned in such a way that she will still have access to the bathroom at reasonable intervals.

If we wanted to try to help Kimmy stay in the classroom more, we could even let her redeem unused passes for points in our class reward system. We may not want to do that right away, since we don't want Kimmy to feel like she shouldn't use her passes, but once Kimmy gets the hang of it, an incentive might help her consider if she really does need to go or not.

TL;DR: Sometimes a student asks to use the bathroom frequently for genuine need, but sometimes that request is a way to avoid working, take a walk, get a moment out of the classroom, or combat boredom. If taking a quick walk to the bathroom satisfies those needs, maybe that's OK. But a system to limit time away from learning activities helps the student be present in class more.

Chapter 5

Busting Classroom Management Frustrations: Disruptive Behaviors

This can be a complicated one to unpack since there are so many reasons a student might be disruptive. Since we aren't covering *major* behavioral issues in this book, in this section, we'll be looking specifically at the collection of small behaviors that distract a student or his peers from being focused on their learning.

Let's take a look at some of the common ways disruptions can manifest.

Getting Out of Their Seats

I teach middle school. That means that, by the time students get to me, they're pretty well trained in the typical behaviors of school. (Bless you, elementary teachers. On behalf of all secondary teachers, I would like to thank you for the work you do preparing students for the basic skills of "doing school." Thank you.) That means I find myself both startled by and ill prepared for this particular issue.

When we returned to in-person instruction during the COVID pandemic, I would go to my desk to take attendance, turn around, and promptly *freak out* because a student was *right there*. I naturally have a pretty big "bubble," meaning I don't typically get physically in other people's space or welcome people into mine. I'm not a Seinfeldian "close talker." And during the pandemic, we were trying very hard to stay an appropriate distance from each other.

But Kimmy was always *right there*.

I don't have much patience for this.

Even if it weren't during a pandemic, this wandering the room would bother me. When a student gets up to find me anytime they have a thought, it presents a couple pretty important problems:

1. She is not likely trying very hard to find a solution herself. In fact, Kimmy would get up to ask me questions before reading any directions, looking for any answers, or using any resources. She wanted me to do the work. I wanted her to do the work.

2. It prevents other students from getting the valid attention they deserve. If I'm with another student, addressing their needs, and Kimmy comes up to us, I now have to divert my attention and give my attention to Kimmy. Again.

Talking Out or Talking Over the Teacher

Students talk. They are, as we've established, human. Human beings are—at least in a biological sense—social creatures. Young adolescents, like the ones I teach, are typically even more drawn to social connections than students younger than them.

All this to say, I know they're going to talk. I do my best to build in opportunities for social learning. If you're familiar with my Boredom Busters, you know I definitely support giving students opportunities to talk about what they're learning.

But what about when students talk out inappropriately? What about when a student thinks every thought that runs through their head is just so revolutionary and so groundbreaking that it just *must* be shared? What about when a student has such poor impulse control that they aren't even fully aware that their voice is on? Or the students who, as I saw on #TeacherLife, learned to whisper inside a helicopter surrounded by chainsaws?

I have two students this year, Brayden and Callum, who just don't have an accurate sense of how much they talk. Both are engaged and do participate in class, so some of the talking out is on topic and really is insightful but offered in a less-than-desirable way. However, both are what some may call social butterflies. Both seem to question their existence if they cannot hear the sound of their own voice.

And both believe I'm unfairly singling them out when I redirect them to be quiet.

You know the look: eyes wide, mouth agape, hands splayed out, palms up, often accompanied by a gasp, grunt, or OMG (or worse), often followed by something muttered under their breath to those around them (further pulling *those* students off task too).

Bothering Others

When Callum found out I was writing about classroom frustrations, he volunteered, "So you're writing about me?" He's a neat kid. He watches the Science Channel for fun. So do I. We've had many conversations about our favorite shows: *What on Earth?* and *Mysteries of the Abandoned*. He is able to remember almost everything he's seen on shows like this and other documentaries he's watched, and he makes intelligent and thoughtful connections with what we're covering in class. When some students in class started reading the book *Grenade* by Alan Gratz and this student found out it covered the Battle of Okinawa, this student shared what he had learned about Desmond Doss from what he'd seen on Science Channel. As a sixth grader, this student was having a thoughtful conversation about pacifism, heroism, ritual suicide, and the true cost of war. That's the thing—in this case, his misbehavior is *not* a symptom of disengagement. In fact, he is often *so* engaged that he just can't contain his enthusiasm.

Why, then, was this student so often turned around or leaning back into other students' space, touching their belongings and generally driving them bonkers?

Let's walk through the flowchart together to unpack what we know about classroom disruptions and explore what we can try.

The Chronic Disruptor

A typically quiet student talking out is not necessarily a symptom of a problem. Instead, it's likely just evidence of humanity (and may even be a very good thing if that student has been too shy to participate or has struggled to connect with others). So in this flowchart, we're looking at how we respond when a typical chatterbox talks out or a room-wanderer gets out of their seat.

Let's take my student Kimmy the wanderer as an example. Here we see that most students *can* continue learning even if she's out of her seat, so we can try ignoring it. Kimmy doesn't escalate—if I ignore her, she just stands there, looking at me, until I address her. But it's also not going to go away. Kimmy will keep getting up and keep standing there, over and over again. Since seat-belting Kimmy to her seat is not an option, let's see what we can do.

When I analyze what's going on, it's clear this isn't a systemic issue—other students are staying appropriately seated and know what they may get up for without permission (sharpening pencils, getting tissues, etc.) and do so without any kind of significant issue.

That means Kimmy and I need a plan.

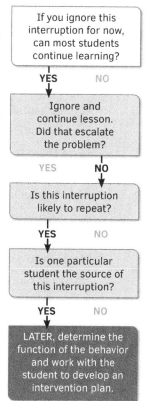

If you ignore this interruption for now, can most students continue learning?

YES   NO

Ignore and continue lesson. Did that escalate the problem?

YES   **NO**

Is this interruption likely to repeat?

YES   NO

Is one particular student the source of this interruption?

YES   NO

LATER, determine the function of the behavior and work with the student to develop an intervention plan.

Talking out often, turning around and bugging neighbors, and getting up frequently can all be the result of impulsivity the student is having trouble containing. You know these students—when they get up and you ask them what they're doing, they look confused, almost like they have no idea how they even got there. They seem to materialize in other parts of the room unexpectedly and without warning. To some extent, this is Kimmy.

In this case, here are some possible strategies we can consider:

- Making sure the lesson is "chunked" in such a way that we are changing gears after any sustained attention, that students get to move as part of the lesson, and so on.
- Providing movement through seating—wobble stools, rocking chairs, and wiggle cushions may allow enough gross motor movement to give these students a healthy outlet.
- Include opportunities for students to talk as they learn. If we expect learning to be silent, all period, all day, we will just find ourselves frustrated as we deal with inevitable talking out. The human drive to socialize is natural. Rather than fight against it, let's channel it.
- If that's not enough for some talkers, establish ways they can share their thoughts without disrupting others or commandeering each class discussion. Maybe you keep a dialogue notebook where they write their thoughts during class. Either they turn it in to you for you to comment back, or they keep it on their desk and you periodically stop by and contribute. Maybe you keep a shared file on Google Docs. The format isn't what's important. The aim here is to give them a less disruptive way to share their thoughts. These strategies are also helpful for students who like to share a personal story in every class discussion.
- If they want to contribute to every discussion but at the expense of other students having the opportunity to participate, maybe they get a set number of comments to use each day. Whether

it's a card they turn in or using a dry-erase marker to tally on their desk, this tangible prompt may help them weigh their contributions more carefully and help them see and understand their boundaries better. Bear in mind, too, alternative discussion formats may allow *all* students to participate in discussion more equitably—discussion boards, chats, collaborative brainstorming spaces, and other similar approaches may also be good fits for these students.

- For students who frequently leave their seats, use floor tape to mark a space around each student's desk to show them where they may move without permission. Allow them to stand, pace, or do whatever they need within their space. Yes, this might be noticeable to other students, but it allows this student to move within boundaries that they can *see*, helping them make more controlled decisions about their movement and behavior.

- Give these students a set number of passes to get up each period. If they want to get up to ask you something, they must turn in one of their passes. When their passes are out, they cannot get up without permission again. This also helps them have a concrete connection to their movement.

Remember Kimmy? What if Kimmy isn't just out of her seat because she's impulsive and likes to move? What if Kimmy is also avoiding the work in some way? Callum was fully engaged in his learning, but was Brayden? What if Brayden was talking out to try to avoid the work? Then we may need to also consider some strategies that address their *learning*.

- Ensure the work is of an appropriate level for the student and that she has the scaffolded supports, accommodations, and other interventions to meet her learning needs.

- The pass idea also works well for these students. It lets them ask a few questions, but once their passes are out, they must try to find a solution themselves.

- For our frequent movers like Kimmy, you can try an "ask three before me" strategy, but be careful to specify that the student must ask only students seated around them so they are not wandering again, and monitor closely to avoid exhausting the patience (or affecting the focus of) students near them. This strategy also does not encourage the student to stop and think first.

- After giving directions, stop by the student's desk. Have her repeat directions back to you or read them to you. Review the resources with her. Do the first problem with her. Then tell her she may not ask you any questions until you return. She *must* try on her own first. Schedule when you will return (say, five minutes), and then she may ask questions at that time. Gradually extend the time until she is working independently for more appropriate lengths of time. In fact, you can apply this to the whole class—everyone must work independently for five minutes without teacher support, using resources and strategies themselves. Then pause everyone at five minutes and allow students to ask questions. Reset the clock and have them get back to work.

> **TL;DR:** If a student is repeatedly out of his or her seat or talking out, offer strategies that allow appropriate movement, socialization, and contribution to discussion, and change the way these students may ask questions or seek support to build up their ability to work independently.

The Escalator

In this example, let's look at my chronic disruptor.

In those first moments of a disruption, most students can probably continue learning. The student creating the disruption and the classmate they're disrupting, however, cannot. I don't like that temporarily ignoring the situation is also ignoring the fact that a student cannot focus. However, it may be best to continue the flow of the lesson for now and address these students in a moment.

In the meantime, we can try some subtle things to redirect our students while we're still teaching. We can move closer to them, even teach from their desks. We could place a hand on the disruptive student's desk and pat it to signal that they need to sit up and be in their own space. But we may not want to call this student out more overtly than that right now—that would derail focus on the lesson for *all* students.

When I have a moment to go over to address this more privately, it communicates to the student the disruptive student was bugging that I saw what was happening and

> If you ignore this interruption for now, can most students continue learning?
>
> **YES**   NO
>
> Ignore and continue lesson. Did that escalate the problem?
>
> **YES**   NO
>
> Can this interruption be solved quickly?
>
> YES   **NO**
>
> Is one particular student the source of this interruption?
>
> **YES**   NO
>
> LATER, determine the function of the behavior and work with the student to develop an intervention plan.

want her to be able to focus. It communicates to my disruptor that I'm trying to address the situation respectfully.

We know this behavior is likely to repeat, so I'm back to arranging a plan with this student. Much of what we've already discussed to resolve talking out or getting out of one's seat or incessantly talking out will work here too. Maybe we make a box around this student's seat so he can more objectively tell when he is and isn't in someone else's space. Maybe we provide a rocking chair so he can rock his chair back safely and without leaning against the desk behind him. We are thoughtful about where we place him in the room and who he is seated near. We look for opportunities to build in social learning and leadership opportunities so he can meet his need for socialization more appropriately. We can give him a notebook or set up Google Docs for him to record his stellar thoughts so he doesn't turn around to share them with the classmate behind him. We develop signals he can agree to and recognize so he knows when he needs to be redirected. From now on, he'll know what that pat on the desk means.

A bottom line I will want him to agree to: Everyone in this room has the right to learn. Any behavior that violates that right, for himself or others, needs to be addressed.

Is any of this going to cure the problem? No. We have to work hard, employing combinations of strategies and responses, observing the results and changing them up, to try to keep mentally active students like this engaged. Thinking of Callum, though he exhausts me sometimes, he's so totally worth it. I love that he loves learning, and I'm honestly impressed by the connections he's making. Compliance does not necessarily equal engagement, and the converse of that is that a lack of compliance does not always mean disengagement. He's engaged. I have a responsibility to try to channel that appropriately so other students can be engaged too.

For these particular students, it's *really* important that they feel respected and heard, and whether accurate or not, they feel disrespected when I have to redirect them multiple times in a class period. The strategies we've covered so far address the disruptive behavior and give the student potential outlets for their thoughts and movements. But one challenge I faced was getting them on board to participate in these strategies. At first, these students all believed I was unfairly singling them out. If I didn't honor those feelings, these students would not likely buy into whatever plan I tried to develop and could even start to push back against me more publicly. My response may actually escalate these students.

I have a point system already established, and it includes a deduction for talking out. That deduction did serve as an effective on-task reminder to these talkative students. But the unfortunate side effect was that Brayden would get angry at losing points and start talking out in retaliation. That's *not* helpful.

My goal became getting Brayden to recognize his own behavior so we could partner together in whatever strategy we would try next. One thing we can try when a student doesn't believe us about their behavior is to do a timed observation where we tally how many times we observe their behavior in comparison to their classmates (or the number of unsanctioned comments vs. sanctioned). This provides evidence to support our claims. These are good tactics to help steer the conversation away from our word vs. theirs. There are even some really good conversation-tracking tools online to help you map participation in a visual way for our chronic talker students, helping us open classroom discussions up more equitably.

We considered potential exacerbating factors. We reevaluated the seating chart and considered proximity to me, guarding against visual stimuli, and being mindful of who they are placed around. Both Brayden and Callum readily admitted they would talk to an empty room, though, so we knew that wasn't our perfect solution.

You've seen the memes. You know what these kids do to seating charts.

With Brayden, the plan we agreed to was that I'd use a certain color Post-it Note as a way to communicate to him that he was talking out. I just quietly place one on his desk as I walk by during a lesson. We established that he'd have to trust me, that when he saw that Post-it, he really *was* talking out.

This really did work well . . . until the other students noticed.

"What's that for?"

"I want one!"

"If you're giving out stickers, can you get Star Wars ones?"

It can be a challenge to deploy a strategy in such a way that the very thing that would help minimize disruption doesn't create disruption itself. We don't want to draw unwanted attention to the student or single them out in front of their peers. We've already seen how counterproductive that can be! There's the challenge of helping the student recognize their behavior, then a bit of trial and error to find the right fit for the student, but there's also the challenge of creating a classroom culture of inclusivity and personalization that normalizes strategies that allow all students to engage fully in their learning.

We've already identified several strategies that may be a great fit for a student like Brayden, giving him opportunities to share his thoughts more appropriately and making sure he's equipped to engage in the learning activities appropriately. But if Brayden doesn't *believe* he's talking out in the first place, he's not likely to engage in any strategy we try. And consequences may be counterproductive since he just believes his teacher is picking on him. Our goal is that a student like Brayden learns to identify his behavior and is equipped with strategies he can use to self-regulate and participate in his education more appropriately.

> **TL;DR:** When an individual student chronically talks out, disrupts classmates, or wanders the room, our response can actually escalate the student. We need to help them more accurately perceive their behavior so they are our partner in whatever strategy we deploy.

The Escalator–Attention Seeker

What if, instead, the disrupting student were hosting *America's Got Talent* in the back of your classroom? What if, instead of getting out of their seat to ask you 4,927 questions, they're taking the scenic route around the room, talking to other students, putting on a show? What if, instead of just being off task themselves, their goal seems to be to disrupt as many students as possible?

This would be a BIG deal to me. When we look back at the functional frustration assessment, I *know* I'm triggered by behaviors that get in the way of other students' learning.

Then our flowchart might look more like this:

We'll see the disruption means most students cannot continue learning—the student has caused a major distraction. We can still provide a quick, temporary solution—telling the student to sit down, moving to their seat and hoping they get the hint, asking them to step in the hallway a moment, and other strategies. But we all know that's not the end of the story. These quick solutions just get us back to learning as quickly as possible—they do nothing to fix the underlying problem. That student is going to materialize beside you again in approximately thirty-seven seconds, or turn around and start tapping on their neighbor's desk. The problem will repeat.

If you choose to send a student to the hall, please be cautious. Many schools' safety plans do not allow students to be in the hallway unsupervised. Removing a student from access to their education is also

If you ignore this interruption for now, can most students continue learning?

YES   **NO**

Can this interruption be solved quickly?

YES   NO

Do the quick solution now and resume learning. Is this interruption likely to repeat?

YES   NO

Is one particular student the source of this interruption?

YES   NO

LATER, determine the function of the behavior and work with the student to develop an intervention plan.

not appropriate, even if they've been disruptive. Remember, these are children. That's easy for us to forget. If you send a student to the hall in this scenario, I encourage you to do it just to remove the distraction so you can get the class back to learning (and get a handle on your own feelings) and then step out as quickly as possible—within a couple minutes—to talk to the student one-on-one. Reiterate that they were not "kicked out of class"—instead, you were removing a distraction so that other students could focus, and you were giving yourself a moment to make sure you are calm and can be respectful toward the disrupting student. Be prepared—they may try to save face in this moment and may not be very receptive (or respectful) just yet. Set clear expectations for what should happen when they return to the room, and make the right of all students, including this one, to learn the highest priority.

The good news is, whether a student is just quietly seeking *your* attention or is out of their seat to seek the attention of others, the same strategies work pretty effectively for both. Later, we have a more appropriate and in-depth conversation with this student and discover it sounds like he's seeking peer attention. Perhaps the student lacks the social skills to seek attention appropriately. Perhaps they just really like the attention of others. Some of strategies we can consider here:

- Make sure this student understands the impact of his behavior on others. If a student has been seeking attention because his classmates are his friends and he likes them, he may obey class rules and expectations more if he understands that he's causing a distraction, and may be more likely to temper his behavior to avoid negatively impacting his friends and classmates.

- Ensure your student has the social skills to seek attention and connection appropriately. Arm her with some phrases she can use to connect appropriately with her peers. Are there clubs or groups she can join? Is there a kind student you can seat her next to so that we can incorporate more social learning into our lessons and she gets to feed her need for socialization more appropriately?

- Consider ways to give this student influence and importance appropriately. Can they have a role within the class or in a group-learning activity? Can you train them on an activity and let them lead a small group as a "resident expert"?

> **TL;DR:** When students are seeking peer attention, they will find a way to meet that need, whether appropriately or not. Make it a priority to preserve the learning of all students, and offer more appropriate outlets for peer attention and leverage that need for powerful leadership.

Beyond Socialization

If socialization isn't the motivation for a student's disruption, it's possible this student is hurting or angry or even feels (and I say this cautiously) "stupid" and is acting out as a result of those feelings. Emotions are complex, and students' brains are still in development, so they're still developing the processes needed to appropriately identify and deal with what they're feeling. If this is the case, this student may not respond to the interventions listed so far. It might be time to show grace, address them privately instead of in front of peers, and tag in the school counselor or other resources. We know challenges like this have a significant impact on learning and behavior. Sometimes the best thing we can do for a student is to show them we don't love them any less when they're messy, and to get in the mess with them so they're not alone and we can help them learn how to climb out of it.

> **TL;DR:** If a student is disruptive because he's dealing with anger, trauma, or challenging learning needs, he might not be able to appropriately manage himself yet. He needs to see we're safe and he's safe. Tag in the team and love him.

A Disruption Epidemic

Chances are high that a student who is disruptive in one way is also disruptive in others. These students can change the dynamic of an entire class. Whether it begins with one or two students talking over others, getting out of their seat, or chronically invading others' space, before long, other students may follow suit and the classroom can devolve into everyone turning around and wandering and talking willy-nilly.

One final possibility to consider is weakness of our own classroom structures. What if, in the case of my wanderer, Kimmy isn't the only one out of her seat? What if you look up from working with a student and notice three other students out of their seats, conversing with other clusters of students? What if, while you're working with a small group, the rest of the students are milling about like particles of a gas in a science model?

Like we need more gas in middle school.

Y'all.

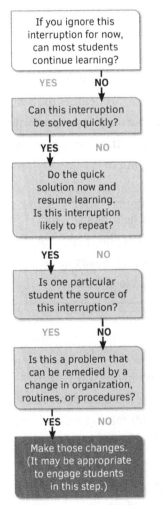

If you ignore this interruption for now, can most students continue learning?

YES   NO

Can this interruption be solved quickly?

YES   NO

Do the quick solution now and resume learning. Is this interruption likely to repeat?

YES   NO

Is one particular student the source of this interruption?

YES   NO

Is this a problem that can be remedied by a change in organization, routines, or procedures?

YES   NO

Make those changes. (It may be appropriate to engage students in this step.)

Now this is a problem that involves the entire class, so we have to approach it with system-wide solutions to address and prevent this problem. If you hold a class meeting with your students, you're likely to find they understand the expectation of staying seated and are aware they are breaking that rule. It's possible, now that it's being discussed openly, that they will agree to simply follow this procedure. If not, though, help them focus on the right of all students to learn and how this behavior violates that right. Help the conversation center around respect for others and the importance of learning rather than the violation of arbitrary rules.

If needed, your students can help you develop a plan. I caution against rewarding compliance with a basic expectation, but it's possible some tangible goals with contingent rewards can help temporarily. You may also offer the whole class some of the strategies discussed above, such as working independently for five minutes and then taking a break to ask questions. Students tend to buy in more when they are part of developing the solution.

Here are a few system-wide solutions you can try to disrupt disruptions in the classroom:

- All hands raised. All students raise their hands for every question asked. If they are confident in their response, they use a straight arm. If they are uncertain, they bend their arm at the elbow. If they don't think they have a clue, they put their hand to their head. The educator extraordinaire Andrew Maxey has all students raise their hands. If they are confident, they raise their left hand; less confident, their right.

- Students can have colored cards (I've seen this done with cups too) that they display on the desk to indicate when they have a statement, question, or need, like the call light to summon a flight attendant on a plane. This nonverbal strategy allows all students to signal that they need attention without getting up or interrupting others.

- There are some tech tools that allow students to enter a digital line when they have a question or something to say. Some are as basic as chats (which we've grown more familiar with through pandemic teaching) or as sophisticated as ClassroomQ, an online system that helps manage student participation and questioning.

- Randomizers: all students think of or write an answer, but you pick a student at random to call upon. Maybe you draw a student's name out of a can of popsicle sticks, or you can use an online student-picker tool. The tool isn't what's important here—the value of this approach is that *all* students answer and know *anyone* can be called upon.

- Require brief silence before anyone responds. This enforces not talking out or disrupting others, and gives students a moment to gather their own thoughts before other students offer theirs. Follow up with any other sharing strategy.

- Turn-and-talk, One Minute Mingle, and other strategies let all students share their thoughts with another human being, even if not with the teacher. For turn-and-talk, students simply turn to a student nearby and share their responses. One Minute Mingle similarly lets students share their thinking but provides an opportunity to move. Students get up and walk the room for one minute, sharing their answers with each other before returning to their seats. I have found, though, that my students who *really* like to talk still want to tell me their answer. If I don't want to call on them from the front of the room or risk them talking over others, I can make sure I meander over to them and let them tell me their thoughts during the conversation time.

> **TL;DR:** Letting a few talkers go too long can lead to verbal chaos in the classroom, and a chronic wanderer may inspire others to do the same. If the whole class is getting in on the disruption, hold a class meeting to get back to the basics, brainstorm solutions, and move forward together. Reconsider what systems you have in place what needs to change so that all students can participate appropriately.

Fads

Sillybandz, the bottle flip challenge, fidget spinners, VSCO girls, Fortnite (and now TikTok) dances—what did you feel as you read that list? Whether you view fads as invading marauders poised to wreak havoc on your classroom or an opportunity to leverage pop culture to engage your students in new and exciting ways, fads do sometimes pose classroom management challenges.

My point here is not to tell you which side of the fad debate you should be on. You are the expert educator in your classroom, and you have every right to establish boundaries you're comfortable with when it comes to fads. But no matter how you feel about these temporary fixations, they *will* impact your students, and you are likely to have to figure out how to deal with them.

I take brief video clips of normal class moments frequently and share these clips with parents and families on ClassDojo. Now my Timehop app takes me on a daily tour of these past moments. The other day, I watched a clip of my students playing an online quiz game. As my camera pans the room, it catches a couple students "flossing" at their desk while waiting for the results to be revealed.

Disruptive?

No, not really.

But if they "flossed" in the middle of direct instruction? Yeah, probably.

That's the challenge with fads . . . they aren't consistent. Some fads don't impact us instructionally or managerially at all. Mom jeans come to mind. I may not understand why this unflattering style is back—and being worn by fourteen-year-olds—but it doesn't impact my role as teacher at all. Others, like Hydro Flasks only affect the classroom environment when they tumble off a desk or get left in a locker. The bottle flip challenge, Sillybandz, and fidget spinners definitely caused more classroom disruptions. I think the varied nature of fads requires us to consider the flowchart on a case-by-case basis, not even on a fad-by-fad basis. That said, I'll use a specific fad scenario from my own classroom as an example for us to work through.

When Fads Disrupt

I wasn't prepared for slime to enter my classroom. I had assigned a passion project where students could research a topic of their choosing and create a Flipgrid "channel," like a YouTuber, to teach us all about that topic. We worked on how to narrow our focus to a target audience, how to reach and engage that audience, and how to keep viewership up. Students analyzed and reflected upon their work. The academic side of it was great.

But you know what a lot of my students were passionate about? Slime.

Instead of opening a can of worms, I'd apparently opened a box of baking soda, several large jugs of glue, and more glitter and food coloring than any classroom not labeled by the term "art" should have.

At the conclusion of the project, students asked, "Mrs. Powell, can we still bring slime to class?"

Here's what my initial flowchart would have looked like:

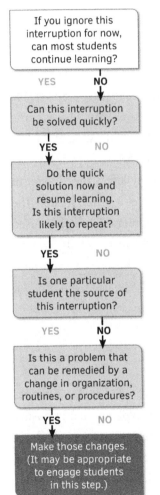

If you ignore this interruption for now, can most students continue learning?

YES   NO

Can this interruption be solved quickly?

YES   NO

Do the quick solution now and resume learning. Is this interruption likely to repeat?

YES   NO

Is one particular student the source of this interruption?

YES   NO

Is this a problem that can be remedied by a change in organization, routines, or procedures?

YES   NO

Make those changes. (It may be appropriate to engage students in this step.)

This was not a one-student issue. Students who had never heard of slime before—having grown up in the post–*You Can't Do That on Television* Nickelodeon show era—were now fascinated by it. They wanted to touch it. They begged students to make it for them. Several students had rather lucrative side hustles going. I had to make a decision. Fast.

Here's what I did. The flowchart takes me to the point of having to figure out a system-wide solution to address this problem for the whole class. Instead of me doing that myself, I issued their next assignment: research and develop an argument answering, "Should Mrs. Powell allow slime in class?" We agreed that whichever side scored the highest average would "win."

The nos won.

But the students raised such valid issues in their essays, we weren't done yet. Students talked about the impact of stress on students. They found statements from child-psychology experts who talked about the fact that since modern generations spend so much time on screens, they lack tactile stimulation. They were so dedicated and sincere, I followed up with a new challenge: problem-solution essays. I told them they'd identified valid problems, so now they needed to map out valid solutions.

The result of that assignment lives on in my class today. Our classroom is gamified, and students can earn customizations to their class experience, like the right to bring a snack to class or listen to music on their own device while they work (see chapter 10 for more on how I use gamification in my classroom). These power-ups are divided into levels by how hard they are to earn. Students decided slime should be a power-up at a level high enough to indicate students had demonstrated reasonable responsibility, conduct, and effort prior to earning the right to use slime in class. They set parameters for use and logical consequences for abuse of the privilege.

Brilliant. Engaging my students in solving the problem of slime in class was one of the best things I've ever done.

And it's worked.

Now it's not uncommon to see a student flipping a sheet of slime out to make a giant bubble on their desk while following along with a text, or running their fingers through a pile of slime while taking a quiz. Students know the boundaries and respect them. A potentially problematic fad became a leverage point for some very powerful—and lasting—learning.

> **TL;DR:** Some fads really do affect the whole class. We're likely to have more successful buy-in from our students if we involve them in the solution (and that solution doesn't have to be as simple as "Yes, I'll allow it" or "No, I won't.").

Disrespecting the Teacher

The final classroom management frustration in this chapter is a very significant one. I've disclaimed before in this chapter that all the frustrations covered in this book are minor, everyday irritants, not big, significant behavior problems. Therefore, it's valuable to define what I mean by "disrespecting the teacher" for the purpose of this chapter.

"Disrespecting the teacher" could mean:

- Eye rolls
- Scoffing
- Muttering under the breath
- Mild work avoidance or delay
- Mild verbal pushback

More significant disrespect, such as shouting, openly calling the teacher inappropriate names, physical aggression, or leaving the classroom without permission would be classified as major and should be handled according to your school's behavior policy. If you would like my input on such behaviors, feel free to reach out to me on Twitter (@beyond_the_desk) or by email (teachbeyondthedesk@gmail.com).

I also must be very clear about something before we proceed. I avoid making blanket statements like, "All teachers should," "You should never," or "Always . . . ." I believe very passionately in respecting your professional expertise, freedom, and creativity. It is OK for two teachers to handle the same thing differently. Both teachers can do so well! Both responses can be right.

However.

I believe it is critically important that students feel respected by their teacher. I believe earning the respect of each of our students should be one of our first priorities and is one of the most important things we can do. In my own experience, a student who feels respected by their teacher is more likely to participate, give effort, behave appropriately, and even come to school. Students who feel respected by their teacher respond better to correction and are more likely to make a sincere effort to participate in corrective plans.

But perhaps you don't trust my experience. That's quite all right. I am, after all, just one teacher, and my own experience may be an incomplete glimpse of reality. Let's take a moment to explore some empirical evidence together.

A *Review of Educational Research* analysis of forty-six studies found the same positive benefits for students that I found through my own experience: improvements in academic achievement, attendance, and behavior.[1] In addition, a study published in the *European Journal of Psychology of Education* found benefits for teachers—teachers who reported positive relationships with their students experienced more joy in their work.

In "One to Grow On / Respecting Students," Carol Ann Tomlinson says, "Perhaps the most powerful attribute a teacher can attain is respect for students."[2]

Where teachers tend to define respect as compliance, students instead define respect as "basic recognition of your humanity."

Consider this: the Stanford University social psychologist Jason A. Okonofua gave two groups of randomly divided veteran teachers articles to read.[3] One group was given an article emphasizing the role of empathy in the classroom, and the other group read about punishment and teacher control. Then both groups were asked how they'd respond to a minor classroom disruption like a student throwing away trash at a less-than-desirable time. Those who read the article featuring empathy were more likely to say they'd talk to the student privately. Those who read about control were more likely to say they'd remove the student from class, involve an administrator, or contact the student's parents.

Over throwing away trash.

We would remove this child from his access to learning because he threw away trash.

That student will likely return to class at some point, right? I mean, no matter how mad his teacher is, he's not likely getting expelled for this infraction. How likely will this student be to participate, be engaged, and give his best for this teacher now?

Can you see why this matters?

We all get frustrated. That's the point of this book, after all. But how we handle those frustrations can and does have an important and lasting impact on our students—the human beings we are responsible for.

It is my professional opinion, therefore, that building a relationship of respect with your students is of critical importance. It should be more important than any academic standard or procedural initiative. That respect is the foundation we're going to build everything else in a school year upon. I believe in treating our students with respect even if they don't respect us. I'll say this in bold: **our students do not have to earn our respect.**

They *do not* have to earn our respect.

We must treat them with respect even when their behavior, attitude, participation, or any other quality makes us *feel* that they don't deserve it. We must treat them with respect because they are the child and we are the adult. We are in a position of power and influence over them, and that relationship *will* have an impact on them. Do we tell our own babies we'll love them when they show us they love us first? We will show them we respect them, that they can trust in that respect, and we will work our tails off to earn their respect in turn. We will do everything in our power to ensure that every student feels safe and valued in our classrooms.

Every. Student.

That relationship can take a long time to develop. Students entering our classrooms with trauma, attachment issues, prior negative experiences at school, heck, even a bad morning will have walls up we must try again and again to convince them to take down. It's not their fault what's happened to them. It's not their fault they are an imperfect human being in development.

We should do everything in our power to convince them that we will treat them with respect.

Phew. OK. Look, I'm tempted to apologize if that offended you. I am. I mean, it's not comfortable for me to give any of my opinions as if they're objective truth that everyone should agree with. And I know my view here challenges a long-standing mindset in education. But, y'all, the research is behind it.

Rooting Out Disrespect

Now that I'm climbing off that soapbox, you may be wondering why I'm covering disrespectful behavior from students if I believe we can earn their respect by respecting them first.

Well, because they're human. And so am I.

There will be times a student plumb doesn't like what I decide for him. There will be times a student had a really bad morning and takes it out on me. There may be times I've had a really bad day and respond badly to a student. There may be times a student pushes back against me to "save face" in front of her peers.

So, yes, disrespectful behaviors still happen in a classroom that values mutual respect. Sometimes those disrespectful behaviors are still pretty major. But research supports that cultivating a relationship of empathetic respect with our students influences both their behavior toward us (and their academic progress) and the way we respond to their behavior.

Let me tell you about Calvin. Calvin came to us midyear. His move was the result of a custody change he was *not* happy with. Calvin had diagnosed behavior disorders and learning disabilities. Calvin had a history of behavioral infractions from his previous school.

Calvin came to us *mad*.

In those first weeks with Calvin, I wasn't focused on his academics. I encouraged participation and employed every strategy at my disposal, but Calvin had walls up like layers of iron coats. I was not getting through. And Calvin was acting out to show everyone just how unhappy he was with his circumstances.

My colleague and I both felt instinctively that the way we responded to each minor situation was crucially important. We both believed that if we messed up and violated any trace of trust Calvin was considering with us, we'd lose him forever. So we were patient. We tolerated some things from him we wouldn't from other students. We worked with him one-on-one. We grouped him with students thoughtfully, kids who were patient, outgoing, warm, and genuinely nice. Little by little, Calvin started to warm.

I remember the day I was working with Calvin at my small-group table. He was going over some problems he'd missed recently and was struggling to understand. He threw his hands in the air and yelled, "If my mom wouldn't have done so many drugs when she was pregnant with me, my brain would work better, and I could *get* this!"

Oh. Oh, Calvin.

In that moment, he was just a small child dealing with big, complicated feelings, processing very real things that were entirely out of his control.

But did you see it? Calvin trusted me. He let me in.

Calvin developed a really close friendship with a couple guys in our classes. We saw him warm up, start joking around more, participating in class, and even getting really excited over his success.

Earlier this school year, one of those boys in Calvin's friend group died in a car accident. My colleague and I stationed ourselves in the conference room of our school, ready to be present with any of our former students who were grieving this loss. Calvin was, understandably, shocked. We really worried about him. We knew Calvin's past trauma would have a significant impact on how he handled this loss and that this loss could set him back.

But something beautiful happened.

Calvin became the leader, taking care of other kids who were grieving. Instead of being sent out into orbit, adrift, Calvin became the center of gravity that eventually grew brand-new friendships.

We still see Calvin every day at the end of school. He always gives us a big, enthusiastic hand-over-the-head wave.

And, you know, I've had dozens of Calvins over the years. Kids whose parents have died under horrific circumstances, kids born into addiction, kids facing homelessness and insecurity, kids abused and violated in unspeakable ways. You don't always know who they are. And the reality is that all kids are susceptible to small traumas every day. Their best friend won't talk to them. They realize midmorning they forgot deodorant. They have to change in the locker room later. Their crush is dating their best friend. Their parents fought on the way to school. Their older brother is drinking too much. They don't have the "right" brand of shoes. You can't always tell who's experiencing trauma. They might be polished, trendy, well-behaved. They enter our classrooms, loaded and vulnerable. And trying to learn algebra or conjugate verbs.

So what do we do?

The great thing is, if we treat *all* students with compassion, empathy, and respect, we'll be doing right by *all* of them.

Let's take a look. Let's imagine that Calvin has shoved his paper across his desk and laid his head down. He's refusing to pick up his pencil and just grunts at me when I try to talk to him. What do I do?

First, I need to check myself. Because I work so hard to build relationships with my students, I'm particularly vulnerable to *this* feeling:

This made me feel:
- ☐ like my students don't like me
- ☑ like I was losing instructional time
- ☑ like this is never going to get better

I can't say exactly why the opinion of twelve-year-olds matters so much to me, but yeah, this one can cut deep. I'm going to do my best to do what's right for Calvin, though, even if he doesn't particularly like me right now. So let's unpack this behavior.

I use the term "ignore" this time carefully. We don't "ignore" a student in trauma. If the disrespect is because a student is saving face or just a little angry with us, ignoring isn't all that risky. But if the disrespect is because of loaded trauma, we definitely notice and keep watch. We just don't address it immediately because then all students in the classroom could become voyeurs to this student's private experience.

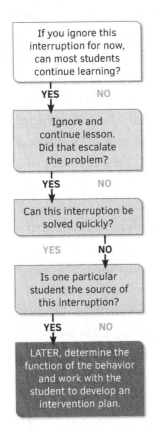

If you ignore this interruption for now, can most students continue learning?

YES   NO

Ignore and continue lesson. Did that escalate the problem?

YES   NO

Can this interruption be solved quickly?

YES   NO

Is one particular student the source of this interruption?

YES   NO

LATER, determine the function of the behavior and work with the student to develop an intervention plan.

It's why you may notice a student quietly crying in the back of the room but get everyone started on page 171 before you go talk to her. You're granting her as much privacy as you can.

So we get the class moving and go over to Calvin. If Calvin is just mad at me, I can establish some clear expectations and give him a moment to feel what he feels. That may sound like "Calvin, I see you're mad at me. You're allowed to feel that way. I'm going to give you three minutes to feel what you feel, and then I'll come back to check on you. By the time I come back, you need to have started number one." Or it could sound like, "Calvin, I see you're mad at me. I'd like to better understand why. Would you step out into the hall with me so we can talk about it?"

If Calvin is dealing with other factors, though, Calvin might need my support. That might look like "Calvin, I see you're feeling big things right now. You're allowed to feel that way, even though it might not feel good. That's OK. I'm right here with you, and I'm not going to care about you any less just because you're not happy right now. I'll sit right here beside you. When you're feeling more ready, I'd love to do number one with you."

One other strategy that is powerful when students push back, for pretty much any reason, is choice. The Conscious Discipline program has a strategy I've used for years, both as a parent as a teacher, called Two Positive Choices.[4] Choice gives the brain a feeling of control, which can be very helpful when someone is dealing with factors that feel beyond their control. Often our knee-jerk version of choice is "You can choose the right thing or the punishment," or "You can do this the easy way or the hard way!" Yeah, that's not helpful. Instead, we offer two equally acceptable options. "Calvin, I see you're feeling big things right now. You're allowed to feel that way, even though it might not feel good. I'm here to help. Would you like to start on the first problem or the last problem?" Conscious Discipline recommends that you keep repeating and offering those same choices until the child responds. I try my best to "read" my students in these moments. Maybe they need me to walk away for a few minutes and then try again. Maybe they need to employ some breathing exercises or focused relaxation first. But, in the end, Two Positive Choices often works.

And it is respectful.

So the next time Calvin feels big things and finds me right beside him, is he likely to push back or comply?

Respect lays a foundation we can build everything else upon.

> **TL;DR:** Students are going to disrespect us sometimes. But a calm, clear, safe response from us lays a foundation we can build better things on.

These disruptive behaviors definitely cause us frustration. That frustration definitely affects us, professionally and personally. As we work to unpack our response to these situations, it's important that we not lose sight of the *student*. The behavior is disruptive, not the student. If we take the time to better understand what we are feeling as we navigate these disruptions in our classrooms, we are better equipped to partner with our students in more effective solutions.

Chapter 6

Busting Instructional Frustrations

In the previous chapters, we unpacked various classroom management frustrations. In this chapter, we'll focus on frustrations of an instructional nature, those challenges related more directly to teaching and learning than classroom procedures and rules. Of course, there's plenty of overlap among any of the categories I've used to organize frustrations in this book. But in a broad sense, these frustrations are the frustrations of effort, work completion, and engagement.

Those of us who taught or led schools through the COVID-19 pandemic know these challenges well. In the spring of 2020, my colleagues had students they hadn't seen or received work from in three months or more. COVID-19 muddied the waters of what constitutes truancy and made these situations difficult to remedy.

I didn't have this kind of truancy in the following school year, but my primary instructional challenge is what I view as the misuse of our online classes. Meant to be for full-time elearners who learn from home due to significant health risks or students under quarantine, we livestream our classes just like so many teachers around the world have done. In the week of writing this, though, I've had students join online because they overslept, fell off a hoverboard, or admittedly didn't want to come to school. I've never encountered incomplete work like I have through virtual and hybrid teaching. Trying to gather all student work is like trying to catch popcorn popped on a stovetop without a lid. While wearing oven mitts. And I'm blindfolded. And maybe someone spun me around seventeen times or so first.

And—ding!—someone just joined the Google Meet.

(Y'all, I'm going to have an elevated heart rate when I hear that particular tone for years to come. The other day, I accidentally tapped my finger against the bottom of my drink tumbler in such a way that the resonant tone exactly matched that sound from Google Meet, and I, no joke, broke out in a momentary cold sweat.)

Like the unique challenges of teaching within the COVID pandemic, the instructional frustrations covered in this chapter do not necessarily have easy solutions. Their causes are complex. But rather than feeling like issues such as a lack of motivation or apparent apathy are beyond our control, we will explore ways to regain some control over these challenges and lessen our frustration.

Not Turning In or Completing Work

There's a lot covered by this one topic. Sometimes students do the work but don't, for whatever reason, turn it in. Some students don't do the work. Sometimes we're referring to homework. Sometimes we see this even with in-class work.

Not Doing the Work

Let's look first at when a student isn't doing the work. This particular frustration always reminds me of Christopher. Christopher was sullen and withdrawn. He spent much of class, day after day, doodling geometric drawings in the margins of his paper but writing little more than his name at the top. This was hard to catch—his pencil was up and moving, so while I was working with other students, a quick scan of the room left me assuming Christopher was working.

He wasn't.

It didn't matter if it was in-class work, homework, a test, whatever, Christopher was unlikely to do it.

Let's examine this situation using our documents.

First, I need to get a better handle on what, exactly, is happening.

This made me feel:
☑ like my authority was being challenged
☑ like I was a bad teacher
This occurred:
☑ during independent work
☑ during partner/group work
☑ when I was busy with something else

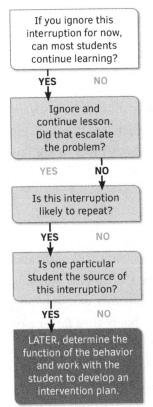

One of the biggest things I noticed when I unpacked what I felt about Christopher's doodling was that I felt like I was a bad teacher. I thought Christopher would *want* to participate in the awesome activities I'd planned. Yet while I was busy facilitating those activities for others, Christopher was quietly opting out.

Then I can use the flowchart to figure out what I can *do* about it.

Unpacking this scenario, I see that I can probably keep class going until I have the opportunity to address Christopher privately. Because most students are working just fine, I have no reason to believe what I'm asking students to do is somehow unreasonable. Once I've got the rest of class going, I can go address Christopher one-on-one.

I tried an important first step: Could Christopher do the work? Just because the task was appropriate for the rest of class doesn't mean it was appropriate for him. I would sit next to Christopher and ask him to do a problem with me. He would be reluctant to try. He mumbled and didn't raise his head much. He was compliant—this wasn't disrespect—but he was clearly not engaged. I ascertained that Christopher technically had the ability to do the work but significantly lacked confidence and engagement.

The next step of the flowchart is to develop a plan with him. Because Christopher was so withdrawn, he really struggled to engage in the planning process. We did, however, agree to try a couple things.

1. Christopher would get to work with one of his only close friends in my class. I established boundaries with this boy so he would understand what working together does—and doesn't—look like. It was important to me that Christopher be the one to do the work, not the other boy.
2. After getting the rest of the class started, I would work the first problem with the boys together. I would also check in more frequently than I might typically with other students.

These steps weren't perfect. Christopher had some mental health challenges his dad was diligently following up on, and some of Christopher's withdrawn nature was definitely wrapped up in this. The companioning with his friend, though, helped. Little by little, we saw Christopher warm up. For a while, more than the academic score he was earning, I was observing Christopher for less tangible signs of well-being—I wanted him to be OK as a human being more than I wanted him to be able to write a compound or complex sentence.

A few weeks after starting these steps, I had to modify an assignment on the fly because our whole school lost internet access, and the version of the assignment I'd planned was no longer possible. I had students illustrate how a character in the novel we were reading had grown throughout the book. For the first time that school year,

Christopher sat up straight, and his pencil was flying over the page—doodling for a purpose now—without starting the assignment with me or working with his partner.

Channeling my inner Gru from *Despicable Me*: "Lightbulb!"

Now we had a new strategy at our disposal: whenever reasonable, I could give Christopher the option to represent some of his work artistically. When I needed more concrete explanation, Christopher could write or explain to me out loud. This accomplished two more things:

1. Christopher had some choice, and like we've said, choice is good for the brain, especially when the brain feels stressed. This particular choice engaged Christopher's artistry, which made him happy.
2. Christopher and I spent more time talking together as he explained his work, and that built the relationship of trust between us.

I'm pleased to report Christopher continued receiving excellent mental health care and came out of his shell, so to speak, more and more throughout the year. He's imperfect, and so am I, so he did not do *every* assignment *every* time. But he produced enough work samples that I was able to assess mastery, provide feedback, and generate some momentum.

> **TL;DR:** When a student isn't doing work even when given time in class, consider ways to engage the student enough to build some momentum. Partners, alternative versions of the assignment, and extra teacher support might get the ball rolling.

Incomplete Work

If the not-working scenario isn't quite like Christopher's, there are other possibilities we can consider. The student might be essentially engaged, or at least compliant, but not organized enough to keep up with homework.

- Is the student using an agenda? Do they have one? Do they know how to use it?
- Do they know where the assignment is listed in the classroom?
- Do they have a folder or another system for storing and transporting assignments?
- Are assignments and supplies making it into their backpack, home, back in their backpack, and back to school each day?
- Does the student have the time to complete the assignment? Setting up a consistent after-school homework routine is helpful. If the student does homework at the same time and in the same place each day, they are more likely to keep up with the work.

> **TL;DR:** If a student is compliant but not completing the work, organization or time management are the likely culprits.

Missing Work

What if we got a student like Christopher to the point that he was actually *doing* the work, but he still wasn't turning it in? This scenario has always baffled me as a teacher. Why in the world would a student *do* the work and then *not turn it in*?! And yet this happens. Frequently.

If we use our flowchart, our path looks the same as it has for each of the single-student scenarios above. We see this isn't an issue that interrupts much of the class, so we can deal with it privately with the student involved. In this particular scenario, if the student is *doing* the work but not turning it in, we are likely again facing a problem of organization. Between home (or wherever they're doing the homework) and the next day in class when they could turn it in, they've lost it.

Our solutions, then, should focus on organization. We can look at ways to help this student not lose their assignment. Or we can look at our own organizational structures to consider if there are other ways we can allow them to turn their work in. Some ideas to consider:

- If this student is losing his assignment sometime during the school day, can they turn all assignments in to their home-room teacher first thing in the morning, with that teacher passing them along to the other teachers?
- If the student is finishing the work at home but losing it before they return to school, do they have a consistent routine at home to make sure they're leaving home with everything they need at school? Can the student load their backpack immediately after finishing their work so they don't leave assignments on the kitchen table anymore? Could their family support them in this?
- If home organization is not successful, could the student turn the work in digitally so they can submit it the moment it's complete?
- Does this student have folders and other supplies and know how to use them? Are their locker and backpack organized in a functional way?
- Do they understand how to turn work in in each of their classes? When each teacher has a different method, students might get confused or not understand how to submit their work. Maybe one teacher uses a tray and another collects assignments from students at their seats. Some may tell students to turn work in; others may assume students know they're supposed to and never remind them. Our student might need clarity to navigate these systems.

> **TL;DR:** If a student is *doing* all the work but not turning it in, consider alternative organizational structures that minimize opportunities for them to lose or forget the assignment.

An Incomplete Work Epidemic

What if, instead of one or two Christophers in a class, or maybe three, max, we have half a dozen or more? What if we're seeing larger-scale work completion issues?

First, let's imagine we have several students not turning in homework.

In this scenario, most students are working appropriately, but ignoring the problem isn't likely to make it go away. We're going to have to address it. This is not a problem with just one student, either, so we need a solution that will work for the whole class. Anyone in education knows "homework" is a loaded word. As we've discussed, this scenario could mean students are doing the homework and not turning it in, not doing the homework at all, are losing it, are disengaged, or more. It's a *lot* to unpack.

Maybe it's time to survey our students, via Google Forms or some other means, to find out why they aren't turning in the work. Maybe we can offer solutions like rearranging class routines to provide more in-class work time, a way to turn work in digitally instead of physically to help students turn work in immediately instead of keeping it until they return to class, providing a more consistent turn-in system, more choice

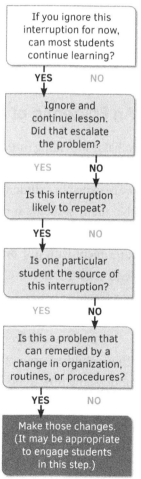

about what to do for homework (say, letting students choose five problems from a set of ten), or trying out a new way to grade homework like homework quizzes.

In this homework quiz strategy, instead of collecting the homework every day, pick three to five questions from the homework to use as a bell-ringer quiz the next day. All students take the quiz whether they have their assignment with them or not. Students who did the assignment find themselves well prepared for the quiz. Teachers release themselves from the burden of tracking down errant assignments.

> **TL;DR:** If a lot of students aren't doing their homework, we can consider different ways to submit the work, choices as to what work to do, or homework alternatives like homework quizzes.

An Epidemic of Disengagement

What if providing more work time or a different assignment collection system doesn't do the trick? What if the problem is actually that what we're expecting students to do is so boring or holds so little relevance that many students simply aren't doing it?

In this case, most of the class is still working, but this is no longer a problem with just one student. However, this is also not a problem with organization or class routines. Instead, this is likely symptomatic of a teaching issue.

Hold on. Before you get upset with me, let's take a moment.

We teach children. Children typically do not love homework. Those children are not completing their homework even though they understand how to do it, how to submit it, and so on.

Our students are disengaged.

Imagine you tell your class, "I have a HUGE surprise for you!" They squeal eagerly and start guessing what it may be.

Donuts?

A movie?

Extra recess?

A special guest?

"No!" you say. "It's *homework*!"

Right?

If you're seeing a significant slump in work completion, it might be time to freshen things up a bit. You can come up with a new, exciting homework alternative and release it to the students as a (real) surprise. Or you can hold a class meeting to solicit their input and give them the opportunity to generate solutions. With increasing access to technology, growing respect for the role of art and creative expression in all subjects, and really exciting new assignment ideas from the likes of John Meehan, Michael Matera, Matt Miller, and others, it's easier than ever to offer a variety of options for our students. John's first book, *EDrenaline Rush*, shows us how to bring the energy of breakout rooms, mud runs, and amusement parks into our lesson experiences. Michael's first book, *Explore Like a Pirate*, teaches even non-gamers how to utilize gamification theory to engage and motivate students. John and Michael coauthored the book *Fully Engaged*, focusing on the science of engagement through curiosity, wonder, and excitement. Matt Miller is famous for the Ditch That Textbook series. Matt's easy-to-apply ideas help us break out of the more boring traditions to better engage our students in powerful learning.

If you ignore this interruption for now, can most students continue learning?

YES   NO

↓

Ignore and continue lesson. Did that escalate the problem?

YES   **NO**

↓

Is this interruption likely to repeat?

YES   NO

↓

Is one particular student the source of this interruption?

YES   **NO**

↓

Is this a problem that can remedied by a change in organization, routines, or procedures?

YES   **NO**

↓

Can this problem be discussed in a way that both respects and preserves the confidentiality of all students involved?

YES   **NO**

↓

Hold class meeting to determine and enact solutions

Maybe the solution is as simple as allowing students to pick which problems to do from a larger set or the use of learning software that personalizes goals for each student. Maybe we create a choice board or assignment playlist and allow students to choose which assignment to do from a variety of options. Maybe we employ homework alternatives like homework quizzes.

In any case, these new approaches are likely to revitalize students and increase assignment completion.

> **TL;DR:** If several students are in a homework slump, freshen class up with new homework options and teaching strategies to increase motivation and reengage students.

Task Avoidance

Students are great at avoiding work.

They need to use the bathroom. They simply *must* tell you about that dream they had last night. Maybe a splinter suddenly materializes in their index finger. This pencil needs to be sharpened just a *bit* more. What's it look like when I write my name with the opposite hand? Shall I add my middle name? Yes, I think I shall.

Strategies we covered in the previous chapter, when we took a look at students who wander the room, may be appropriate for this scenario as well. In this section, we'll focus not on the obedience of getting started on a task, but on the academics of task avoidance.

Jasmine is a pro at task avoidance. She lays out every color of writing utensil in ROY G. BIV order. She gets up to tell me about her dog or her latest drawing. She adjusts her sweatshirt. Oh, look, she brought the wrong folder. Looks like she'll need a trip to her locker. Jasmine doesn't move terribly fast to begin with, so these small avoidances *really* add up.

Most students are still working, so I can try ignoring this. Maybe Jasmine will just get to work. Often, though, Jasmine can manage to *look* busy the entire work time but accomplish nothing, so this is likely to require intervention. And this problem *is* likely to repeat.

My quick solution might be verbally reminding Jasmine to get to work. I might reference the countdown clock on the board. I might provide whatever supply she's searching for so she can get started. These temporary Band-Aids might move her toward getting started right now, but they didn't address the underlying cause of her task avoidance.

There are a number of really good student interview questionnaires, often used as part of the response to intervention (RTI) process, designed to help us get to the bottom of behaviors like task avoidance, including the pre-RTI team meeting student interview from Jim Wright of Intervention Central. If I pull Jasmine aside and ask her questions about things like how difficult the work feels and what she views as her strengths and weaknesses, I may discover she really doesn't like my subject area or feels like the work is too hard. In my experience, task avoidance is typically due to feelings regarding the difficulty of the work or basic disinterest.

If you ignore this interruption for now, can most students continue learning?

YES   NO

Ignore and continue lesson. Did that escalate the problem?

YES   NO

Can this interruption be solved quickly?

YES   NO

Do the quick solution now and resume learning. Is this interruption likely to repeat?

YES   NO

Is one particular student the source of this interruption?

YES   NO

LATER, determine the function of the behavior and work with the student to develop an intervention plan.

The feedback from the questionnaire helps me design an intervention plan specific to Jasmine's needs. Remember, we aren't talking super specific, multistep plans here. Instead, in this book we're focusing on *minor* irritants and exploring sustainable solutions. So interventions for Jasmine might include:

- Arranging to work the first problem with her to get the ball rolling and then setting expectations from there, such as having two more problems done in the next three minutes.
- Offering Jasmine two positive choices, such as, "Do you want to start with the first problem or the last one?"
- Use of a partner to engage Jasmine socially and in the work.
- Simple rewards like points in the class system for every time Jasmine completes the work in the time provided.

Task avoidance isn't likely to involve more students unless the avoider goes on a performing arts tour around the classroom, in which case the strategies used for a performing disruptor in the previous chapter would be appropriate.

> **TL;DR:** A student who delays getting started may feel the work is too hard or may be disinterested. Employ a quick strategy to get them started.

Not Following Directions

When we moved to virtual learning in the spring of 2020, I discovered I'd created a monster of a problem.

I would type out directions and post them on Google Classroom and Pear Deck. I would post a video of myself going over the directions. I'd even record a walkthrough to demonstrate the directions in action. During live class over Zoom, I'd explain the directions.

And then . . .

Emails, Classroom messages, Zoom chat messages, and verbal requests: "Mrs. Powell, what do we do?" Or my favorite: "I don't get it." (I'm rolling my eyes and sighing as I type this.)

I had apparently conditioned my students to be wholly dependent on me for their directions. Instead of using any one of the many resources at their disposal, I had unintentionally trained them to wait for me to tell them what to do. It was so bad that, even when I told them what to do, they still zoned out, then asked me what to do.

Not following directions can be a *big* problem. It has a direct impact on academic success, since neglecting directions results in improperly completed work.

And it's annoying.

So what do we do?

Some of that depends on whether we're dealing with an individual student or two neglecting directions or a class-wide epidemic like I was.

The Individual Ignorer

We'll start with the isolated cases.

Yes, we can ignore the problem, and *maybe* the student will catch on and turn to their resources. But the more likely scenario is that we'll need to go over the directions with them quickly so they can get busy with the task and we can maintain the focus on learning. We know that's a temporary solution, though, that does nothing to address the underlying problems.

So we'll need to find a solution to address following the directions without disrupting learning. Some possible options are:

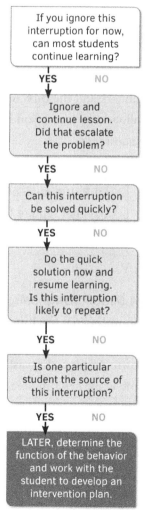

- When the student asks what to do, have them read the directions aloud to us. This requires them to use a resource and actually *read* (or listen to) the directions.

Often they'll get knee-deep in the directions and go, "Oh, I get it now."

- When the student asks what to do, use nonverbal communication like tapping on the directions printed on their page or pointing to the directions on the board and then walk away. Check back quickly, in a couple minutes, to observe the student and see if they've gotten started appropriately.

- Require that, instead of asking you what to do or saying, "I don't get it," the student must ask a specific question about the directions. This requires them to read (or listen to) the directions and *think* about what they mean before asking for help.

With each of these strategies, check back with the student after the first few minutes of work time to ensure they really did correctly understand the directions. Otherwise, they could feel like they aren't allowed to access you if they really do need help or continue the task incorrectly.

TL;DR: If a student isn't reading the directions, employ solutions that require them to read the directions before they ask for help.

A Directions-Ignoring Epidemic

In my virtual teaching situation, though, it wasn't an isolated student or two not using their resources to understand the directions on their own. Instead, the vast majority of the class was leaning directly on me while avoiding reading the directions themselves. This is a different issue.

As we unpack this scenario, we see this issue disrupts learning for the majority of the class, so we can't ignore it. We can offer a quick solution for now so that we can get back to learning, but then we'll have to figure out a better solution from here on out so that we don't have to deal with this every day. This is a procedural issue—we have class routines and tools, but students are not using them.

In this case, our response could include:

- Making sure students really do know where to find directions. Do they know how to navigate Google Classroom and Pear Deck? Do they see where the printed directions and instructional videos are located?

- Making sure students understand the directions. I can have students repeat back to me, in their own words, what they are to do. This will encourage paying attention and will also allow me to get a decent idea whether or not they have an accurate understanding of the task.

- Banning "I don't get it" and "What are we supposed to do?" Instead, like we considered above, require students to ask a specific question about the directions. This might look like "When you say to provide text evidence, are we quoting from the text or paraphrasing?" or "Can I trace today's sight words in marker?"

- Gradual release: Work a problem or two as a whole class. Have students do the next one on their own, but go over it. Then turn them loose to complete the rest on their own. This will

If you ignore this interruption for now, can most students continue learning?

YES · **NO**

Can this interruption be solved quickly?

YES · NO

Do the quick solution now and resume learning. Is this interruption likely to repeat?

YES · NO

Is one particular student the source of this interruption?

YES · **NO**

Is this a problem that can be remedied by a change in organization, routines, or procedures?

YES · **NO**

Is this a problem that can be remedied by a change in organization, routines, or procedures?

YES · NO

Make those changes. (It may be appropriate to engage students in this step.)

demonstrate the directions in action before expecting students to follow them independently.

- If students have printed or virtual directions, have them highlight the actions in the directions. This forces them to be attentive to the directions, to use the provided resources, and focus on what to *do* for the task.

> **TL;DR:** When we've inadvertently allowed bad habits around directions to develop, we need to send students back to their resources instead of leaning on us to rescue them.

Not Wanting to Try When It's Difficult

Growth mindset is now a pretty widely accepted concept. Attributed to Carol Dweck, it posits that struggle and failure are natural elements of progress and that success is more a result of effort than inborn ability. Growth mindset has been part of the education world since the late 2000s.

We may find, however, that some students are afraid of failure. Additionally, some students seem to be allergic to effort.

The Individual Shirker

We joke that my youngest son is like water. He's going to seek the path of least resistance. Though clearly very bright, the work he submits to his teachers is often far below what he is capable of. Partially followed directions, bare-bones responses, and a great deal of whining when effort is required show that my son has not embraced the concept of growth mindset just yet.

When similar whining and declarations of "It's too hard!" infiltrate our classrooms, what do we do?

First, we'll look at how we can respond when an individual student shirks effort.

Again, we see the path where most students are still engaged in learning; ignoring the problem temporarily allows us to keep moving, but we're going to have to face the issue at some point. The student is likely to continue to avoid hard work if we don't do something. So what are our options?

First, let's consider the difficulty of the work. Is it possible it really *is* too hard for the student? If so, we can scaffold in appropriate supports, work a few problems with them to get them going, allow them to pick a few problems from the whole set so they can lean on those they're more comfortable with, and use tools like screen readers and talk-to-text.

If the work isn't truly too difficult, though, encouraging growth mindset is where we land. Some of our same strategies may still work, at least to get the student moving. Working a problem or two with them, allowing peer support, and offering choices might build some momentum. But if the student is still afraid of failure or resistant to giving concerted effort, even these strategies are short term at best.

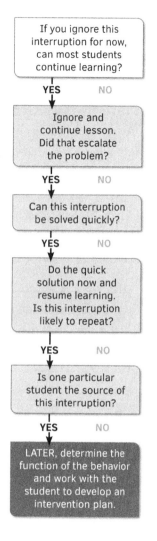

This student may benefit from some way to visualize their effort and progress. Perhaps you show them a work sample from earlier in the year and identify with them how their current work demonstrates growth. Maybe you provide the student the safety of allowing them to correct their assignment after completing it so failure isn't quite something to fear. In my previous book, *Boredom Busters*, many of the Homework Buster activities I included focused on learning from mistakes over grades. A grade feels final, even if the skill isn't yet mastered. Instead, we want the assignment to be part of the learning. When we focus on what went wrong and why, we learn from those mistakes and do better next time. The assignment isn't about the letter grade, then—it really is a valuable step of the learning journey. Error analysis, metacognitive prompts, and more shift the focus from just right or wrong and back onto what we are *learning* from each assignment. (You can find some examples at teachbeyondthedesk.com/grading-homework.)

One other possible solution is to have them rate their effort on each task. Next to each task item, have them score their effort on a simple scale, like 1 to 3. If they gave very little effort, they score themselves 1. If they gave strong effort, 3.

> **TL;DR:** If a student resists giving sincere effort, first ensure the work isn't genuinely too difficult, then help them shift their focus toward effort over grades.

A Resistance Epidemic

Rather than isolated cases of allergies to effort, though, we are often facing more widespread fear of failure and resistance to effort. In a way, I think we've created this. So much of school is about earning certain grades. It's understandable that students now ask if every task is for a grade and play the game of school rather than stepping out to take creative risks, or fear working hard on something they might not succeed at.

That scenario looks more like this:

In this case, the fear of failure and avoidance of effort prevent many students from truly accessing their learning. There are no real quick solutions—we can force students to be compliant, but we can't quickly change mindsets. Instead, we're going to have to do some work to start shifting those mindsets to help them embrace growth and focus on progress over perfection.

One of the most powerful things we can do to encourage growth is emphasize feedback over grades. The concept of feedback over grades in the modern classroom can date at least back to 1958. Ellis Page performed a study that involved observing the results of different combinations of descriptive feedback and grades. The results were clear—students improved more from descriptive feedback than from grades. The most effective feedback is both clear and supportive.

The power of feedback isn't just in the receipt of it, though. Instead, when we have students revise their work using that feedback, they are active participants in their growth and can clearly see the direct result of their effort. Revision is powerful.

Over time, students are less afraid of failure because they know they will receive feedback that helps them grow and will be given an opportunity to put that feedback into action. Students take pride in their growth. Even if a grade is given, students now see the direct correlation between their effort and their score.

In addition to feedback and revision, we can also employ strategies like the Homework Busters mentioned earlier. These activities direct students to focus on the *learning* of the task rather than the grade of the task.

One other interesting aspect of growth mindset is gamification. Experts like Michael Matera who have explored the power of elements

If you ignore this interruption for now, can most students continue learning?

YES   NO

Can this interruption be solved quickly?

YES   NO

Is one particular student the source of this interruption?

YES   NO

Is this a problem that can be remedied by a change in organization, routines, or procedures?

YES   NO

Can this problem be discussed in a way that both respects and preserves the confidentiality of all students involved?

YES   NO

Hold class meeting to determine and enact solutions.

of gaming in education were intrigued by the fact that a person might willingly fail over and over again in a video game and not give up, but will flee desperately from any hint of failure in the classroom. Gamification explores how to bring the motivating aspects of gaming into the classroom to normalize failure and encourage students to keep failing forward. We will explore this more in chapter 10.

> **TL;DR:** To encourage growth mindset, we need to provide feedback and opportunities to put that feedback into action so students can see the results of their effort and growth.

Student Apathy

I initially put off writing this section. Apathy felt nebulous. I was tempted to follow the flowchart straight down the right-hand side, answering "No" to "Do you have any control, power, authority over, or ability to influence the outcome of this problem?"

But I was wrong.

When I started researching apathy in the classroom, I found a blog post by educator Chris Holmes that floored me. On the *Education Post*, Holmes writes about traveling across the country to find out why students are apathetic toward school: "What I heard is the same story: Lack of motivation is always related to having no voice in the classroom, no connections with people or no confidence in their academic abilities." Some students and former students he interviewed broke down in tears as they talked about loneliness, self-harm, and the trusted adults who had given up on them along the way.

There's a moment of encouragement when he says that every student he interviewed talked about there being one teacher they knew who "bent over backward" to support, encourage, and believe in them.

But all of these students also said that one teacher wasn't enough. Holmes then makes a startling claim:

"It's not students who are disengaged, it's us."

He continues, "The next time a kid says 'I don't care,' what he or she really is saying is, 'You haven't given me sufficient reason to care.'"

How, then, do we get them to care?

I've taken a bit of an unconventional approach on this one. You'll notice I didn't follow the route that would land us at holding a class meeting to solve the problem together. After Holmes's post, I just can't. I don't think it's up to the students to fix their own apathy. I think this one's on us. I think we need to back up and re-evaluate where we might be failing—or at least not succeeding—our students and consider what we can change.

Honestly, this feels a bit like a conclusion for all the various frustrations we've unpacked so far. We make sure they can do the work. We honor their need to move, to socialize, to have a voice. We make sure they feel safe. We offer choices. We partner with them.

We respect them.

Will it be perfect? No.

> If you ignore this interruption for now, can most students continue learning?
>
> YES   **NO**
>
> Can this interruption be solved quickly?
>
> YES   **NO**
>
> Is one particular student the source of this interruption?
>
> YES   **NO**
>
> Is this a problem that can be remedied by a change in organization, routines, or procedures?
>
> YES   **NO**
>
> Can this problem be discussed in a way that both respects and preserves the confidentiality of all students involved?
>
> YES   **NO**
>
> Do you have any influence over the outcome of this problem?
>
> YES   **NO**
>
> Take action to address the source of the problem.

But I haven't stopped thinking about Holmes's post. Each of those students said a teacher made the effort for them, but it wasn't enough. But what if we *all* make that effort?

Perhaps that would be enough.

And even if it's not, I want to believe that when my students move forward into whatever future they carve out for themselves someday, a bit of me will go with them. I hope they remember how I sat beside them when they were afraid, stayed with them when they were messy, believed in them when they didn't believe in themselves, and helped them see just how much they are capable of.

A student recently wrote that doing a small thing about a big problem is like laying down the first piece of bread for a PB&J sandwich. She said it's a lot easier to add the rest of the ingredients once that first piece is in place.

You may notice I didn't finish the flowchart this time. I can't. I don't know if this will "work" or not. That part remains unwritten.

Maybe we can't solve the entirety of student apathy right now. But I'm confident we can each do *something*.

When it comes to addressing instructional frustrations like these, we may find it difficult to acknowledge our role in our students' engagement (or lack thereof). But their behavior is communication. What are they telling us? When we listen, we have the opportunity to develop learning experiences that are truly impactful, meaningful, and memorable.

Chapter 7

Busting Professional Frustrations

When I surveyed teacher friends about what frustrates them during the school day, many of them referenced frustrations like paperwork, meetings, extra duties, unreasonable policies, and feeling a lack of professional respect.

I think the reason these frustrations in particular are so demoralizing is the lack of control we have over these circumstances.

Many of the things that frustrate us are also within our ability to influence. We can develop a procedure for student bathroom use during class. We can provide pencils for students who forgot theirs. We can work a student through feedback and revisions until they feel proud of their growth.

Even factors we don't have control over—like a student not being able to afford basic school supplies or not having electricity at home—we can still address. We can gather donations from a local nonprofit to outfit that student with everything he needs, and the student without electricity can plug her Chromebook in as soon as she arrives to school so it's juiced up for the day.

But when a district-wide initiative descends upon us, bringing scads of new paperwork, deadlines, acronyms, and meetings, we typically have no say. The vast majority of the time, no one asked us. The vast majority of the time, no one will. We'll be expected to implement the initiative, to be fully compliant, and as long as we turn our paperwork in on time, no one will ask us how it's going, what we think of it, or what we think we should explore next.

In the same message, we'll be told to make sure we take good care of ourselves and have our paperwork in by 3 p.m.

By the time the COVID-19 pandemic raised the question of whether or not educators could do their jobs safely and forced the world to really consider what we were asking of our teachers, many, *many* teachers had already had enough.

According to a RAND Corporation survey, reported by MarketWatch, of teachers who left the profession before and during the pandemic, three-fourths said teaching was "always" or "often" stressful. That stress outweighed low pay as the reason teachers cited for leaving.[1]

In part 1 of this book, we covered the effects of stress not only on teachers, but on our students. We also discussed the startling cost of teacher turnover. If we are going to keep qualified, effective teachers in the classrooms, we've got to address these high levels of stress and frustration. Many teachers don't feel respected as professionals and feel they have little voice in what's expected of them or how they do their job.

It's my goal for this chapter to help us find what control or influence we can over these administrative and professional frustrations and try to reclaim some of the professionalism many of us feel we've lost.

It is worth noting, though, that this is not a chapter of complaining about our principals and superintendents. We understand these administrators also have initiatives and requirements that come down on them and must filter down to us in some way. We understand that some initiatives are born out of the best of motives and intents. If you are an administrator reading this book, I encourage you to *listen*, so to speak, for how these initiatives can make teachers feel.

Before we begin looking at individual frustrations, I want to take a moment and celebrate the community of educators. Although we struggle to receive the respect our profession warrants in our culture, and even in our own districts, I see the way educators support each other in our hallways and on social media. I see the absolute enthusiasm we lavish on preservice and first-year teachers, the excitement we share with them when they announce their first job offers, as they get to decorate their first classrooms. I see the way we celebrate successes, share good ideas and awesome templates, post notes from conferences others couldn't afford or get time off to attend, podcast our thoughts, and advocate for education to anyone who will listen. Others may not see it. But I do.

And it's awesome.

Lean in. Support each other. Be awesome together.

Addressing Professional Frustrations

As we begin to examine these professional frustrations, it's worth noting that with the exception of some flawed policies that unfairly affect specific student populations, most professional frustrations do not directly prevent our students from engaging in the lesson we're delivering right now. Additionally, though ignoring these frustrations will not make them go away, they do not necessarily escalate the problem. Whatever paperwork we were assigned will still be there after class. Whatever extra duty we've been assigned is still ours when class is done. Temporarily ignoring these problems to focus on the students we have in class *right now* does not usually make these problems worse; it just delays dealing with the problem.

Next, for the most part, these problems are not appropriate to discuss with our students. Yes, there are notable exceptions. Students are affected by some of these same policies and requirements, so it makes sense to help them understand *why* they have to participate in standardized testing, socially distance, leave backpacks in their lockers, and so on. But when I think about a data report I have due or a new professional development program I have to attend, those aren't issues I need to involve my students in. It is to the benefit of my students to feel positively about their school and the structures of the school, and if I pull back the curtain to reveal the peddler projecting the image of Oz, I could negatively influence their perception of their school. It's not appropriate to vent to them or whine about these professional expectations in front of them.

If a policy change *would* have a direct impact on my students, however, our flowchart might descend to a class meeting to discuss the issue and plan how we can respond together. They benefit from being part of the solution and response even if not all the details are appropriate to discuss with them. This opportunity for students to have a voice is actually positively powerful.

For the purpose of this chapter, with the exception of the first professional frustration we'll cover, these issues affect us behind the scenes but do not have a direct impact on our students. Therefore, we are left to consider if we may have any control over these challenges. The answer to that question will vary tremendously from person to person, situation to situation. Within the same building, one teacher might have a position of influence another does not. That same teacher might not have any capacity to impact one problem even after directly impacting another. We can examine some examples together, but it is quite possible in light of this that your own descent down the flowchart will look different from our samples from time to time.

Finally, one terminus of the flowchart directs us to examine the *effects* of a problem even if we can't directly solve the problem itself. This may be where we land for some of these problems. There are many, many challenges in the world of education over which we have no real authority or influence. In fact, when I assess my own feelings of frustration over these professional issues, my results look like:

This made me feel:

☑ like I have no control over this issue

☑ like my authority was being challenged

☑ like I had no say or voice

☑ like this is never going to get better

Rather than be left with that powerlessness, however, we *can* unpack how that frustration affects us in our own classrooms or roles and plan what to do about it. In that way, we can reclaim some power, and maybe even some joy.

Schedule Disruptions

The week we wound up closing our school building due to the COVID-19 virus, we were running an altered schedule due to standardized testing. It was also the week of a full moon. And it was almost spring break. And our altered schedule meant my students ate lunch forty-five minutes later than they were used to.

I already have a poor concept of time. Change my routine even a bit, and I find myself looking at the large, multicolored schedule I scrawled on the board approximately 17,042 times every period. My students who struggle to adapt to change or have executive function deficits might be antsy, nervous, wound up, or anxious. It's like having the left and right shoe swapped for the day—it may work, but it's not quite right.

How many times have you found out your schedule will be changed due to a pep rally, assembly, or something else? It feels like this happens *all the time* in the world of education. Sometimes these disruptions are for happy reasons—opportunities to celebrate and play with our students or learning opportunities we could not provide in our own classrooms. Many times, however, these disruptions are for administering standardized tests or other universally un-fun requirements.

Sometimes we get plenty of advance notice for these changes, and we can adjust our plans accordingly and loop the students in to prepare them. Other times, though, we arrive at school to find out we have to adjust our plans on the fly as students are coming through the door because something vitally important has come up.

This is the one professional frustration we'll cover in this chapter that does have a direct impact on our students and their opportunity to learn in our classrooms. That means this particular frustration has a different flowchart path than the others we'll see later on.

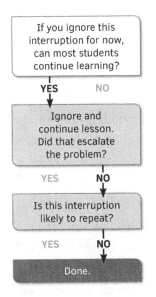

When our schedule is disrupted, as annoying as it can be, the reality is that most students are not dramatically affected; most can continue to access their learning just fine. In the flowchart, the term "ignore" does not mean that we do nothing about the schedule change. Obviously we need to accommodate it. Instead, "ignore" is referring to the fact that we don't need to employ some kind of strategy or plan to deal with the schedule change, and that this change does not somehow escalate. Although interruptions do repeat in the sense that sometimes we have an altered schedule for a few days during testing, or we may have a pep rally at some point again in the future, not employing a strategy of some sort does not cause a schedule disruption to repeat. Therefore, for the most part, though schedule changes are annoying, we can safely take a deep breath, tolerate them, and move on. We adjust our plans and guide our students through the new times, and then life can go back to normal. Yes, these disruptions might irritate us. But the reality is, they are typically highly temporary and will go away without us devoting any more concern to them. In that sense, we can spare ourselves from any additional professional stress over disrupted schedules.

> **TL;DR:** As annoying as disruptions to our schedule can be, they are typically relatively isolated and contained. Rather than employing some sort of grand plan to strategy with them, we can adjust our lesson plans, tolerate the altered times, and then move on.

When Schedule Changes Disrupt Students

There are times, however, that schedule changes significantly disrupt some of our students. In those cases, our chart might look like this:

In this case, if we don't particularly *do* anything to deal with the schedule change, we're leaving the distressed student unsupported, and their reactions are likely to escalate. If we find ourselves in this situation, we can support the student in getting through the schedule changes, but now that we know changes to routine are going to negatively affect this student, we should develop a plan to proactively support them in the future. Whereas before we could analyze these schedule changes as unlikely to repeat, in the sense that nothing about a schedule change one day means it will affect future days to change, we *do* know this student is likely to encounter an altered schedule at some point in the future. Therefore, we develop a plan to help this student navigate schedule changes and have this plan ready to go the next time we face an altered schedule.

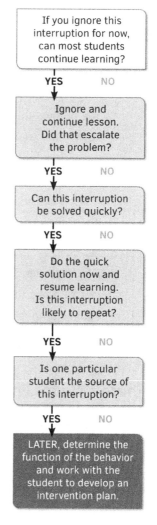

Some possible strategies include:

- Let the student—and their family—know about the change in advance. This can be a tricky thing to time. If you alert the student too far in advance of the altered schedule, the student can stress over it before the change has even happened. Not enough notice, and the student can be left ill prepared. It's likely the student's family can advise how much advance notice is appropriate.
- Provide the new schedule in writing or images so that the student understands when elements of their routine will happen.
- Before each element of the schedule, give the student a moment of notice. For example, just before the bell would normally ring to dismiss class, you can say, "Remember, James, the bell would normally ring now, but today we'll stay in class for twenty more minutes."
- Provide adequate support for the emotions the student may experience. Tools like weighted lap pads, fidgets, breathing exercises, meditation, and more may help a student process their anxiety in healthy ways.

> **TL;DR:** If a student struggles significantly with change, develop some strategies to better support the student through future schedule changes.

There's Never Enough Time

Beyond abbreviated class periods due to special events and circumstances, I'd wager every teacher can agree that there never seems to be enough time.

This is something I've reflected on often throughout my career. From the moment I enter the building in the morning until I finally lock my door to head home, I feel like I'm sprinting. I stay hours past my contracted time and still leave work unfinished on my desk.

Or haul it home with me to do after my children go to bed. Uncompensated.

In the world of education, we don't have enough time to microwave a frozen meal or relieve our bladders conveniently, let alone meet every instructional need that comes our way.

And yet we still have to fill out facility request forms, tick off who has turned in their permission slips, ask the custodian for more disinfectant wipes, enter our data for our professional learning community, contact three parents of students we're concerned about, but—of course—we can't forget to make some positive contacts too.

I have often said that the hardest thing about being a teacher is knowing I've given my best and that it's still not enough.

There's always something unfinished and incomplete.

And sometimes those somethings directly affect the young human beings I'm responsible for.

My friends, it's hard.

Before we unpack this challenge, I want to acknowledge the power of a principal in this conversation. My last principal started teaching at the same time I did. When I first started working in my district as a Title I teacher, I loved being in his classroom. He was the kind of teacher who *saw* all students and made all students feel comfortable in his room. He did trivia challenges and chucked Jolly Ranchers out as prizes. It's something I'll always remember.

When he became our principal, he did everything he could to protect our time so we could focus on instruction. If there was a form to submit to request a bus for an upcoming trip, he did it. If the museum needed a call to confirm our field trip's date, he did it. If the central office requested an analysis of our latest standardized test data, he put it together and even separated it into reports pertinent to each department. If a form the central office wanted us to use was more complicated

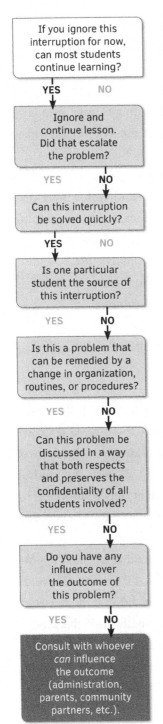

If you ignore this interruption for now, can most students continue learning?

YES   NO

Ignore and continue lesson. Did that escalate the problem?

YES   **NO**

Can this interruption be solved quickly?

YES   NO

Is one particular student the source of this interruption?

YES   **NO**

Is this a problem that can be remedied by a change in organization, routines, or procedures?

YES   **NO**

Can this problem be discussed in a way that both respects and preserves the confidentiality of all students involved?

YES   **NO**

Do you have any influence over the outcome of this problem?

YES   **NO**

Consult with whoever *can* influence the outcome (administration, parents, community partners, etc.).

than he thought it needed to be, he'd advocate for a streamlined approach.

The result of his effort was that I felt respected as a professional. I was able to spend more of my very limited time planning effective instruction, working with students, or contacting families instead of filling out paperwork. I know his own to-do list must have been very daunting by taking so much on, but we were so much better for it.

Even with this administrative support, there still wasn't enough time. And we all know this kind of administrative support is, dare I say, rare?

So what do we do about this feeling that there's just never enough time?

I've chosen to unpack the issue of time this way. In the barest sense, the lack of time does not prevent my students from learning. I can ignore it in the classroom, and my students move forward just fine. But the problem isn't going to go away. For the most part, this is not an issue that can be remedied by some kind of procedural change on my end. Sure, I can take steps to make sure I'm as effective as possible in my prep time. But the problem of lack of time as a teacher is not one I can solve by establishing some procedure in my classroom. I've also decided here that it's not appropriate to take this problem to my students. I don't think they need to know the details about the administrative responsibilities on the periphery of teaching. That's not their concern. It doesn't directly affect their learning. I also believe very few teachers have any real power or authority over what's being asked of them. Instead, the action we can take is to consult with whoever *does* have that kind of influence.

I can't, however, determine what will happen next. If I went to my principal now and said, "With all due respect, sir, I'm having trouble keeping up with _____ and _____ responsibilities," he would ask questions to find out more about why and either offer a compromise or even arrange coverage for my class at some point so I had some protected time to catch up.

I know, he's the goose that lays golden eggs. Try not to hate me for it.

> **TL;DR:** If we do not have any influence over the volume of administrative tasks asked of us, we can have a conversation with someone who does. Ideally, a fair compromise or protected work time could be arranged.

Approaching a Time Crunch without Administrative Support

It is possible that admitting to having trouble keeping up could, unfortunately, reflect poorly on you or damage a needed professional relationship with your boss. I hope that's not the case, but I acknowledge it's a possibility.

If that conversation isn't possible—or is possible but not productive—we wind up at the terminus on the far right: deal with the *effects* if we cannot influence the actual problem. Below is an incomplete list of possible effects of a lack of professional time and what we can do about them:

If we find we have little time to keep up with planning, we can thoughtfully coplan with another teacher. Exchanging this workload or dividing it among us lightens the load each of us carries (and probably introduces us to new ideas).

Another possibility to expand our planning opportunities would be to tag in the students. We've avoided involving them in our time issue since it had no direct impact on their learning. But *planning* their learning is an effect of this time issue that *does* directly impact them. Giving students the opportunity to have a true voice in how they learn is a powerful opportunity.

If we find we have little time to keep up with grading, we can employ in-class activities that allow students to evaluate their work as a learning activity. I've included several such activities in chapter 11, and you can find more in my previous book, *Boredom Busters*, or on my website, teachbeyondthedesk.com.

Another suggestion for managing grading responsibilities would be to use online tools that autograde for us. Tools like Google Forms, Socrative, Quizizz, Edulastic, and Formative are free, grade for us, and even provide basic analysis of the results.

I have found it difficult to find time to make individual phone calls to parents and families sometimes. Now, rest assured, I understand the value of a phone conversation over an email or other digital communication. However, if I just need to notify some parents that a particular assignment is missing or give them a heads-up that a project will be due soon, using the BCC feature of our email lets me send one message, privately, to a number of parents or guardians. I'm also grateful for tools like the stories feature of ClassDojo to let me quickly push important information out to families.

When I'm barely keeping my head above water, I *definitely* don't have time to seek out and read current educational research. Instead, it might help to sign up for one or two thoughtfully selected newsletters to receive a brief overview of new research findings and exciting new strategies right to my inbox. Two I love are the *Monday Minute* released by Susie Highley of the Indiana Middle Level Education Association and the *Focus on the Middle* email newsletter from the Association for

Middle Level Education. Since I teach middle school, both offer strategies, articles, and resources cultivated specifically for my grade level.

Protect your planning time. I know, there's real value in shooting the breeze with your coworkers. That sense of community is so important, we'll devote a portion of this chapter to it. However, if you're behind, it may be beneficial to shut and lock the door, lower the lights, and get to work.

It's OK to say no. If you're asked to serve on a number of voluntary committees or contribute to other tasks but aren't given additional protected time to do so, it may be time to say, "No, thank you."

I can't offer a strategy to specifically address whatever paperwork or professional tasks are nonnegotiables from your administration. But hopefully some of the strategies above will help you shave some time off planning, grading, and professional learning so that you have more time available to keep up with the nonnegotiables.

> **TL;DR:** If you *can't* negotiate either more time or fewer tasks, you *can* protect your time in other ways.

Volunteer or Voluntold

Serving on a committee is a double-edged sword. We've just explored the severe lack of professional time in the world of education. Serving on a committee undoubtedly takes more of that already limited time. However, we also just explored this:

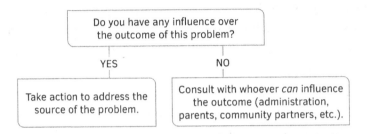

With issues like the demands on teachers' time, we often either don't have the authority over those issues or need access to those who *do* have authority over these issues. Serving on a committee or taking on a leadership role may give you the authority to make change or, at the very least, give you the opportunity to have a voice with those who do have the authority to make change.

In other words, though we clearly need to protect our time, we also need opportunities to shape decision-making that affects our job.

To examine the issue of committee or role appointments, then, we'll take two fronts:

1. How to respectfully say no if you can't take on another commitment.
2. Why serving on a committee may be the right thing to do.

How to Respectfully Say No

There are times we're asked to step in or step up beyond our capacity. Sometimes we're being asked (or told) to serve in a way we're not equipped for or that wouldn't be a good fit for our abilities and expertise. Sometimes we're already extended as far as would be healthy for us. Sometimes we're being expected to serve beyond the contracted boundaries of our jobs, and we have the right to say no. Sometimes our reason is personal and isn't anyone else's business. Whatever the reason, it helps to be armed with some ways to say no so we're ready when we're asked. Here are some suggestions:

- I won't be able to give it the attention it deserves.
- _____ is a bigger priority right now. I need to give that the attention it deserves.
- I appreciate being thought of, but I think _____ may actually be better suited for this position.
- I can't take on anything else right now.
- I've already committed to _____.
- It's just not a good time.
- I've already taken on a lot of leadership roles. _____ might like the opportunity.
- Unfortunately, my schedule won't open up until _____. If I can be of assistance then, I'd be happy to.
- I appreciate you thinking of me, but I'm trying to better prioritize family time.
- I can't serve on the committee, but I can _____.

The intent is to express gratitude for the opportunity—if you're being tagged in, that speaks highly of you—but to speak up for yourself and protect your time. Even if you aren't being asked, even if you're being "told" to take on this commitment, I encourage you to attempt to speak up for yourself. Some schools require committee or extracurricular participation. If that's not the case for you, the person who picked you for the role may think they're honoring you by assigning you to it. They may not realize they're actually overextending you.

> **TL;DR:** If you are asked or told to serve in a role you don't have the capacity for, express gratitude but politely say no.

What if the Right Answer Is Yes?

What if you try and are ignored? And what if great things could happen if you agree instead?

Most of the professional frustrations that discourage and exhaust teachers are issues they have no authority or influence over. It is by serving on committees and in other leadership roles that teachers actually get a say over the running of their schools. If you're given the opportunity to have a voice and have the capacity to serve, you may find it of benefit to you and your colleagues to give it a shot. Either you'll be in a position to make decisions yourself or will have the opportunity to have a voice with those who make the decisions.

> **TL;DR:** Serving in a role gives you the opportunity to influence the decisions made for you and others. This is an effective way to combat the powerlessness many teachers experience.

Meetings

If you have the opportunity to influence the nature of meetings and professional development at your school, please consider doing so.

All of us have endured meetings that should have been an email, hiding our stack of grading under the table and sneaking texts to our best teacher friends. We've all ridden out professional development initiatives that make little sense for our setting or are likely to disappear once the meetings are concluded.

These scenarios are so common, the internet is full of games to liven things up. That reflects the fatigue and eye-rolling feeling we get when the same educational buzzwords get tossed around in every meeting. It reflects the way we often feel PD is something we have to endure instead of a vital component of our effectiveness and growth as educators. PD *is* a vital component of our effectiveness and growth as educators. So as a provider of professional development myself, I need to take a moment to draw an important distinction between effective professional development and ineffective professional development.

Consider this incomplete chart:

Effective Professional Development	Ineffective Professional Development
• Targeted to the needs of staff	• Chosen without input of building leaders
• Differentiated	• One-size-fits-all
• Includes choice	• Not relevant to some members of staff (who are required to attend anyway)
• Relevant	
• Long-lasting	
• Job-embedded	• Goes away after the initiative is over
• Utilizes the strengths of your staff's own resident experts	• Includes scads of paperwork
	• Requires sacrifice of own time
• Engaging	
• Accessible	• . . . boring . . .

We need to stay apprised of current research and new ideas. We need to continue growing and learning as professionals. We need to identify our weaknesses and shore them up. We need professional development. We don't need bad professional development.

I remember that pretty early into my career, the school I was teaching for had scored poorly on the state grading system and we had to participate in a lot of professional development as part of our school improvement plan. We were spending half days out of our classrooms as frequently as twice a week to attend multihour training sessions full of paperwork—and assigned homework. We invested *hours* into these initiatives. We did not pick them. Every staff member attended, whether they taught art or English (though effort was made to divide teachers into "teams" to specialize the program a bit). So. Much. Paperwork.

One morning, I walked in with my computer and grabbed my stack of handouts for the day. As I turned to take my seat, I heard a veteran teacher say, "It'll go away. Just ride it out. Once the meetings are over, we'll never touch this again. We never do."

I was shocked.

Sadly, she was right.

There are a few problems here. One, initiatives like this that are pushed down from above the school don't have buy-in from staff. We can't understand why, of all the things we could spend our time on, *this* is what was chosen. Two, this kind of professional development demands a great deal of our time while also pulling us from our classrooms—repeatedly. We wind up behind in both worlds, our instruction and keeping up with the paperwork. It's discouraging, to say the least. Three, because we couldn't see the grand plan of how this particular initiative fit in the vision for our school, as soon as it was over, it was over.

That just scratches the surface.

In addition to professional development meetings like this, we also have required professional learning community meetings full of paperwork designed to prove we're actually having professional conversations during that time, staff meetings going over announcements for the week, team meetings to discuss concerns about students (where we, again, fill out paperwork to show how we spent our time), etc. We do need to be in professional community with each other. We do need to talk about concerns and develop plans together. We do need documentation to analyze and track what we're trying. But all of these things can be done badly too.

The consequence of having just too many of these valid meetings or even a few bad meetings is that we could find ourselves giving minimum compliance instead of truly connecting with, learning from, and teaming with each other.

And this can have a negative impact on our students.

If you are in a position to make decisions about meetings in your school, I encourage you to help meetings be effective and meaningful by:

- Eliminating any paperwork that is just for proof of compliance

- Keeping meetings brief
- Focusing meetings around a clear agenda
- Maintaining the lens of only doing what's best for kids or what supports staff to do what's best for kids
- Allowing staff a voice in planning meetings

Although the fact that we must attend meetings isn't typically negotiable at all, it is worth remembering these pieces of the flowchart:

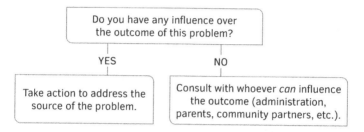

If you have a voice, please use it.

And, remember, if a meeting directly or indirectly supports what's best for our students, it is likely worth our attention and sincere participation.

TL;DR: As annoying as meetings can be, we do need to work together as staff and continue our professional learning. Meetings are done well if we maintain the lens of only doing what's best for kids or what supports staff to do what's best for kids.

Infrastructure Issues

In the fall of 2019, my school was victim of a cyberattack that knocked out our internet for multiple weeks. In addition to the headaches of losing access to the wealth of digital tools I love to use, our phones were tied to the internet, so we also lost the ability to make or receive calls. That meant no calling the office. The office couldn't call me. I couldn't call parents. I couldn't email parents. I was cut off. The icing on the cake was that even our ability to sign in to the copy machines was tied to the internet, so we couldn't so much as make copies.

Fun, right?

This forced innovation, and I was actually quite proud of what I came up with to make life work through that stretch. I was able to deploy some of my favorite busters (as featured in my earlier book, *Boredom Busters*), and since we couldn't even make copies or print, I leaned heavily on hands-on activities, small-group work, and class discussions. Hungry Hippos, Alphabet Soup, Junk Drawer, Paper Airplanes, and more took center stage. Instead of being the activities we used to practice skills, I had to learn to set up explorations and activities to deploy the content as our primary method of learning. It was fun! I wouldn't have taken this approach if I didn't have to. I was forced out of my safe routines in a way that wound up benefiting my students and making me a better teacher.

Then the pandemic hit, and we all pivoted rapidly to virtual instruction.

When the 2020–2021 school year started, my whole district started losing internet connection. Again. This continued in an unpredictable and intermittent fashion for months.

Imagine teaching in a hybrid model and your internet goes out, taking the school's servers with it. That means even students learning from home can't access Google Classroom or any of the resources you've posted there. You can't email them. You can't communicate with them over Classroom. Once again, you are cut off.

I wound up having to plan two versions of every lesson: the version I'd teach if we kept internet, and the paper adaptation backup, shared *somehow* with my online students just in case Classroom went down. I fretted over the inequity of some students not being able to access my instruction or our activities just because they were full-time elearners, so I was reluctant to just move forward with my in-person students when the internet went down.

By February, I'd given up. I plugged a DVD player into my big screen and brought a selection of discs from home. When the internet went down, I let the students pick a movie and pressed play.

When I talked to my colleague one afternoon that month, she asked how I could seem so calm in the midst of all this. I made a box with my hands and said, "Things I can control . . ." then I moved my hands over and said, ". . . things I can't control."

I was losing my mind trying to adapt to problems I had no control over. Putting in a movie bought me some peace.

It was temporary.

When the internet continued to go out in March, I could not justify any further loss of instructional time. I had to confront, again, the fact that infrastructure issues totally beyond my control were directly affecting my ability to teach.

And my students' ability to learn.

You'll notice I've violated several rules of flowcharting here. Let me explain. First, I highlighted both routes through the "Can this problem be discussed in a way that both respects and preserves the confidentiality of all students involved?" question. My thought is that I needn't burden my students with how to solve the internet issues, but they *can* and perhaps should weigh in on how we adapt if (when) the internet goes out. That leads to two prongs of response: one where students help me figure out what to do if (when) the internet goes out and another where I figure out what I can do about the connectivity issues.

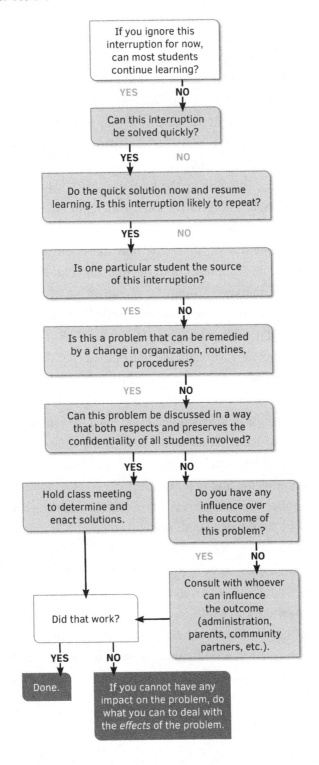

I violated the rules of flowcharting again after the "Did that work?" question. My principal was responsive to our frustrations over all this internet unreliability, but like us, it was really beyond his control, too. However, he did have some influence and lobbied for something to happen. That *did* work . . . for a while. A great deal of effort from a great number of people and organizations has been expended to try to ascertain and resolve our internet woes. Whatever is wrong is so complex that even after being fixed, multiple times, it's still going out. So, yes, his influence on our behalf *did* work. But the problem persists for reasons that are still not understood.

This lands me back at considering how the flowchart can help me unpack and deal with the *effects* of the problem. Even when exerting whatever power or influence we have, sometimes the situation is still beyond our control. When that happens, the frustrating thing is still in our world, impacting how we feel and how we do our job. We loop back up the flowchart to try to preserve learning the best we can despite the frustrating circumstances.

Your infrastructure frustration may not be quite like mine. Maybe your copier keeps jamming, or someone jams it and then flees the scene of the crime. Maybe you have limits on how many copies you can print. Maybe your students don't have consistent access to technology. Maybe your provided teacher device is so old it can't support the programs you'd like to use. Maybe you don't have a way to project in front of your class. Maybe your room is way too hot or too cold. Maybe your textbooks are badly out-of-date. Maybe you're livestreaming your class over Zoom or Google Meet every day.

There are things we *can* control and things we *can't*, but sometimes those things we *can't* directly impact our ability to teach.

> **TL;DR:** When infrastructure issues arise, find a solution to preserve learning for now, exercise whatever influence you have over the problem behind the scenes, and deal with the effects of the problem so learning can continue.

Feeling Isolated

If you are feeling isolated, lonely, or judged, first, I'm sorry. Second, you are not alone. We spend our day surrounded by other human beings but largely isolated from other adults. When we *do* have time with other adults, it's limited and goes very quickly. We may be the only teacher in our content area or have trouble fitting in with the clique of teachers in our building.

We may pour into our students to address their complex issues and many needs but have little to fill us back up. Compassion fatigue is real.

A study into the effects of loneliness in teachers found that the lonelier a teacher felt, the less satisfied they were with their job. That circles us back to the impact of teacher stress and job dissatisfaction on students and on our economy.

This matters.

When I surveyed my teacher friends on social media about what frustrates them on the job, loneliness, isolation, and being judged came up again and again. I remember feeling lonely as a teacher. Early in my career, I was a special education teacher. When you teach a noncore class, you sometimes don't fit. Meetings might group teachers by math or ELA, but where does a special education teacher fit? I was young, new to the profession, and shy. It was hard to connect. Everyone was very nice to me, and I never felt left out. But I did feel lonely. As my confidence as a teacher grew, I developed a new feeling. I wasn't just lonely because I wasn't in a particular content area. I was lonely because other teachers didn't "get" me. Again, everyone was very nice to me. But that's different from fitting in.

Eventually I found pockets of enthusiasm and energy, people that liked their students and were excited to find new ideas. Then, the game-changer for me was attending my first national teaching conference. In 2015, I attended the annual conference of the Association for Middle Level Education. By myself, on my own dime, so I was traveling and attending alone. I took a seat in the general session the first morning, set down my bags, and, being shy, just quietly looked around.

And I was floored.

The energy in the room was incredible. Thousands of people, educators, just as enthusiastic and excited and weird as me, all gathered in one place! I felt energized just by attending, and I came back filled to the brim with new ideas to share back at my school.

One thing I remember from that conference: I walked to the restaurant across the street from my hotel one night to eat dinner. Since I was shy and at the conference by myself, I was also dining alone. I noticed a group of people gathering, hugging, and shaking hands, welcoming more and more people. I could tell some of them were meeting in person for the first time, but they clearly knew each other and were excited to be together. I remember wondering, "How do people do that?"

Later I found the answer: they met on a Twitter teacher chat.

Social media has given us new ways to connect and grow a community not restricted by our geographical borders. Can't find "your" people at your school? Maybe you'll find them online. There is a wealth of online groups, chats, and other gathering points that allow educators to connect over various grade levels, content areas, passions, or needs.

I'm fortunate to have eventually found true friendships in my building. My colleagues are not just the people I teach with—they are my friends.

If you're struggling to find your place at your school, here are some more ideas to help you connect and find likeminded educators to share ideas and support with:

- Find a single shared interest or passion to connect over. Maybe it's escape rooms, or another teacher is really good at Google Classroom tricks, so you can ask them for help.
- Be an encourager. People like being around people who make them feel good.
- Avoid commiserating at the expense of the students. Venting is one thing. Talking about kids in a way that would be national

news if recorded and posted online is not. It's OK to walk away when the line is crossed.

- Join a positive teacher community online. Facebook, Twitter, Instagram, even TikTok have groups of teachers connecting and supporting each other.

- Protect what time you get for your other relationships. Yes, I know there's always something to grade or plan. But if you have the chance to join a friend for dinner, watch a movie with your kids, or take a walk with your spouse, that may be just what your heart needs.

- Stay excited. Fill your professional cup with conferences, webinars, podcasts, publications, and other ways to connect both with exciting new ideas and with the people who are also excited by those ideas.

TL;DR: Feeling isolated or judged is a serious problem. Make an effort to connect with others in your building, but also expand your community by connecting with other educators online.

Feelings of Inadequacy

We're closing this chapter with perhaps the biggest, most significant, most pervasive professional frustration: feeling like we're somehow not doing enough.

Every day, we see so many needs. Each student has their own learning needs, their own history, their own emotions, their own challenges, their own victories. We see colleagues exhausted, bitter, overwhelmed, on the verge of giving up. We plan, deliver instruction, assess, analyze and reflect on results, differentiate and remediate, assess again, and we know we're still coming up short. There are parents we haven't contacted, papers we haven't filed, content we haven't curated, colleagues we haven't supported.

At the end of the day, we haven't been enough.

Anyone feeling that?

I am.

Here's the thing. We're not enough. The needs of any one human being are complex, and we serve multiple human beings a day. We have demands coming in from all sides. What pleases one stakeholder displeases another. We cannot be enough.

Not by ourselves.

Remember those boxes I made with my hands when the internet went down? Things I can control and things I can't. We can't control what happened to our students before they came to us. We can't control what learning challenges they were born with. We can't control what they witnessed at home before they left for school this morning. We can't control if they're sick or well. We can't truly even make them do their work. There are so many variables beyond our control.

We can control what our classroom feels like when they arrive. We can control how we greet them. We can control how we respond when they need to use the bathroom twelve minutes after class starts. We can control how engaging we make our lessons. We can control how connected we are with other educators so we feel fresh and energized professionally. We can control the care we take of ourselves. We can control that we will treat them with respect, no matter what.

We can only do the best that we can do.

At the end of the day, to determine whether we've been successful or not, we can look back over that which is within our control and evaluate how well we've done those things. Where we realize we were short-tempered, impatient, ill prepared, or wrong, we can unpack the situation, identify needed change, and try again.

After all, that's what the functional frustration assessment and frustration flowchart were designed to help us do. Today, if you are feeling like you've failed, I encourage you to pick one of the frustrations we've covered. Start at the top and follow your perspective down.

Where does it lead you? What can you try differently? Make a plan so you won't be caught unawares next time. Try again.

And, please, lean in. Find a friend, maybe even an educator friend, and vent your heart. Seek real feedback but also real support. Don't let yourself go this alone. The community of educators is wonderfully diverse, creative, resourceful, and supportive. Reach out, connect, and grow. If you can't find someone, reach out to me (on Twitter at @beyond_the_desk or by email at teachbeyondthedesk@gmail.com). You are not alone.

> **TL;DR:** The honest reality is that we can't perfectly meet every need we encounter every day. Too many things are beyond our control, and the needs are just so many. But we *can* work hard to meet the needs within our control. This frustration-busting process is one way to do that.

One of the biggest sources of frustration for teachers is the feeling that so many things that affect our job are beyond our control. Sometimes that's not really the case, and when we unpack the problem, we find that there are things we can do to create positive change. Even when something *is* beyond our control, though, there *are* things we can do to mitigate the effects of those frustrating circumstances on our students and keep the focus on the learning.

Part 3

Big Ideas to Bust the Frustration Before It Even Starts

I love sitting in the sunshine.

My heavy English, Irish, and Welsh heritage means I don't come anywhere close to tanning. I'm so pale I'm practically transparent. In fact, I'm pretty sure I can burn just *thinking* about the sun too much. My affinity for sun, therefore, has nothing about tanning. Instead, perhaps I'm part plant. That feeling of warm sunshine on my skin . . . it's almost like I can feel my very cells soaking it up, storing it away for darker days when I may need it.

There's a Kid President quote I have on a Post-it Note by my computer: "Things won't always be awesome, but your response can be." This book has been about those not-awesome times. We've acknowledged the cost of frustration upon us and our profession. We've identified our feelings. We've figured out how we can respond when we're frustrated, both to patch the situation up to get us through and how we'll face it next time. We've explored the extent of our power and influence and how to do the best we can with what we can. We've committed to not being in the darkest days alone.

But we also need turn our faces toward the sun, soak in the brightness and warmth, fill our cells and our souls, and store it away for darker days when we may need it.

For some of us, it's been an awfully long time since we've felt the joy in teaching. We need to find the joy.

Earlier in this book, I talked about how the best offense against frustration is a good defense. In this section, I'll share with you some of my favorite joy-inducing and frustration-reducing strategies and approaches.

I'd like to offer a disclaimer, though: in no way am I saying *this* is how you should teach. As I've said before in *Boredom Busters* and my public presentations, you are the expert in your classroom, and one of the most beautiful things about our profession is that there are so many ways to do it well. You can—and perhaps should—reject any ideas that don't suit your circumstances, philosophy of education, teaching style, or interests unless presented with definitive evidence as to why such a thing is critical to doing your job well. I do assure you that everything I'll offer here is rooted firmly in educational psychology and neuroscience, especially adolescent development, since I have spent most of my career in the middle grades. At the very least, perhaps something I offer here will spark an idea of your own and lead you back to a bit more of that joy.

Chapter 8

RELATIONSHIPS FIRST

At the start of each school year, my primary objective isn't academic, at least in the sense that you won't find it on any standards list. Instead, I try hard to earn the trust of my students and help them learn to trust each other. I teach reading, and most students feel very vulnerable as readers. If you survey students, even many of those you think of as proficient self-report that they are "bad" readers. Especially as students enter early adolescence and become more and more aware of social hierarchy, students can be very uncomfortable reading, and potentially failing, in front of their peers.

But I need them to read. So I have to work hard to earn their trust but also to help them learn to trust each other. Because of that, every activity I plan in those early weeks is specially designed to establish not only the procedures we'll lean heavily on all year but also to create a culture of safety, acceptance, and community.

Here are a few of my favorite ways to do that.

Learning the Ropes

The first day of school, I often have students "break in" to our grade level. Essentially a breakout or escape room, I launch a series of puzzles and clues through which students will learn about how our class will run, what I'm like, what we'll cover this year, and so on. This is a far more engaging way to go over this important content than me just reading it out to them, and students see from the get-go that I do things a bit . . . differently. As they work together and excitedly share clues, they get a taste of how great it can feel to work together as a team.

Once they solve it, we get to celebrate together. It's a great way to launch a year!

Additionally, I use my favorite Hungry Hippos and Paper Airplanes Worksheet Busters from my previous book, *Boredom Busters*, to discuss our summers, pose and answer questions about our new school year, and get to know each other.

Defining Class Values

In that first week of school, I also have students identify how they want to *feel* in our class. Over the next couple of days, we spend time exploring the descriptions they name and narrowing our list to a handful of clear, powerful words we recognize are important to us. Because students don't always understand what we mean by "values," I explain to them that we "value" feeling this way. These values then become the standard of how we—me included—treat each other. We post these prominently in the room. Rather than a list of rules, we explore how we should behave so that everyone gets to feel safe, respected, welcome, and wanted. Interestingly enough, one value students often name is not feeling rushed. That's one I struggle with: I fill each class bell to bell and keep a pretty intense momentum going, so I have to check myself so I don't violate our values either. Throughout the year, when behaviors come up (as they do) that violate these values, instead of a student being in trouble for violating some arbitrary rule I established because I like things a certain way, they can more easily understand how their behavior affected someone else's right to feel safe, respected, welcome, or wanted. I have MUCH more buy-in with conduct and discipline this way.

One side benefit of establishing values with my students every year is that I get to hear what's important to them. As they submit their initial individual responses to the question of how they want to feel in our class, I learn a lot about my students by what they name.

Facing Discomfort

Finally, as we begin our first academic unit, I intentionally create and include learning activities that gently force students out of their very small comfort zones, often limited by fear and insecurity, and challenge them to bravely risk trusting each other. Again, because I teach reading, my goal is to get them more comfortable reading together so our reading groups can run successfully (and largely happily) all year. We start with a lot of modeling. I read, model think-aloud strategies, etc. Very soon, a few hands start going up with volunteers to read. Soon after that, I can pull a few small groups while others read independently, and I repeat the same pattern in the small groups and soon require every student to read, even just a little bit, aloud. We acknowledge the awkwardness and fear. Something cool almost always happens. When I ask them, in that small group, who is a bit uncomfortable reading aloud, almost every hand goes up (even if they do that close-to-the-chest half-raise thing), and then students realize EVERYONE felt the same way they did! Most students sit there, *sure* they are the only one who feels afraid, and when they realize other people feel that way too, they smile, even laugh, and start to open up more.

It's so important that they see they are not alone, even if it's being not alone in their fear or awkwardness.

Little by little, we get more comfortable reading in those groups. I keep groups the same for those early days so they have a circle of people they trust. Then, when I start to mix the groups up, I keep clusters of kids together in their new groups so they still have someone they are comfortable with as they develop trust with their new group. By the end of our first unit, everyone will have read with everyone else, and though it's not magic, we see that sense of trust extend to whole-group activities and the nonacademic community of our classroom.

Although I include a lot of choice in what students read the rest of the year, I do start us all on the same novel. As the characters make good and bad choices and those choices impact other characters, we have great conversations about real-world issues and the importance of our own character. Kids often find it easier to examine the choices of a character, and then, when called to connect the character's choices to their own, are able to understand the impact of their own actions in a way they often didn't realize before. This gives us a common language, so to speak, that we can refer back to all year.

Fostering Safety in the Classroom

We know students must feel safe in order to learn. That means they must feel safe with me and with each other. But what about when a student feels unsafe within themselves? A couple years ago, I had a number of students who had experienced a shocking degree of trauma. I won't share their details here, even anonymously, because those stories are theirs to tell. But you can replace their stories with your students' own stories, I'm sure.

In any case, the effect of their trauma was definitely impacting their ability to access academics. I had a bit of a kooky idea that wound up working splendidly.

One day, I showed up to school wheeling a bright orange suitcase around. I dragged that thing *everywhere* I went. We competed in an advisory volleyball challenge that morning, and I brought my suitcase onto the gym floor and hauled it around as I tried to hit the ball to help my team. I hauled it across the gym floor, in front of the whole student body, when our school counselor called me over to ask me a question. By then, I had fielded a lot of questions about my orange bag.

I wouldn't answer any of them.

By the time we settled into class, my students were beside themselves:

"What's in the bag?"

"Did you bring us something?"

"Are you traveling somewhere?"

"Is it heavy?"

I'd only answer, "What do you mean?"

Throughout class, my bag came with me. When I sat down to take attendance, my bag was there. As I instructed from the board, my bag was securely against my calves. When I circulated among groups, my bag followed. When I supervised passing periods and bathroom breaks, the bag came with me. If a student offered to help me with my bag, I refused. I insisted I could manage by myself.

By the time it was almost the end of class, my students were *bursting* with curiosity. Finally, I said, "Have any of you noticed my bag?"

Duh.

I asked them what they thought it was about. They suggested I was traveling, or I had something valuable, or I was cooking up some big surprise.

Then I asked them, "What if my bag is a metaphor of some kind?"

Some of them started to get it. "Mrs. Powell, do you have some baggage?"

Aha.

I explained to them that everyone has baggage—we all have experiences we haul around with us every day, everywhere we go. I explained that we carry important things, things we need or find valuable to us, in baggage when we travel, and the figurative baggage we carry with us is important too. Even if that baggage became ours through a bad experience, it's *our* baggage, and that makes it important. I told them it's OK to hold our baggage close. But I also asked them if my baggage got in the way at all that day.

They laughed. I had tried to play volleyball with my baggage. I tripped over it *far* more times than I'd like to admit. They watched me struggle to carry other things and my baggage all day.

Yes, my baggage had gotten in the way. I asked them if sometimes their baggage gets in the way too.

Yes, yes it does.

We talked about how sometimes our baggage is just too big and too important to let go of. We have days, like the anniversary of a parent's death, where we hold our baggage really close to our hearts and don't want to let it go. That's OK. Sometimes our baggage is more important than reading, writing, or math.

Baggage Check
Need to put your baggage
down for a minute?

Tap here to set it down.

I asked them if I'd ever needed help with my baggage today. Again, they chuckled at me. I'd obviously needed help many times. So we talked about how sometimes our baggage is just too heavy or unwieldy for us to manage on our own. We talked about who our safe adults and support systems are and how they can help us when we find our baggage just too heavy to carry on our own. But I also challenged them—I told them there were times they could tell I needed help but that I had never sought help on my own. In fact, I had refused their help. "There will be times safe adults and trusted friends in your world can see that you need help," I told them. "When that happens, trust them."

Finally, I asked them if all baggage is the same. We started with the concrete example of all the different kinds of bags we can carry. Then we segued into the different kinds of emotional baggage people carry. I picked up my suitcase and hefted it a couple times. I'd filled it with dictionaries that morning. It was heavy. I asked a few students to try hefting it. I asked them if it was heavy. Some said yes, but others claimed it wasn't heavy at all.

"Our baggage is like that," I explained. "What's heavy to me may not be heavy to you, and vice versa. It can be tempting to compare our baggage to someone else's and judge what they find difficult. But baggage doesn't work that way. If something is hard for someone to carry, it doesn't matter if we would find it easy to carry that same thing. What matters is that it's hard for them. We need to see that, respect that, and offer our help."

Sometimes, though, that baggage gets in the way when we want and need to engage with the world around us. Sometimes we need to set it down. But that can be scary. Those experiences are personal to us, and it can be really hard to set them aside, even if for just a while. So we established "baggage checks" in the room, a spot on the door and a spot on the table where I work with students, where students can tap the baggage check to metaphorically set their baggage down for a bit. It will still be there for them to pick back up later if they need to.

From then on, it was common to see students pass my table on their way to the pencil sharpener and tap the baggage check or tap the one on the door on their way in. Many immediately latch on to the value of this tangible way to set aside intangible feelings and challenges. Other times, though, I might notice a student struggling and suggest we go set the baggage down together. When a student would tap the baggage check, they knew what it meant. I knew what it meant. It was a way to tell our brains, "Yes, I feel this big thing. But right now, so I can focus on other things, I'm going to set it down."

I won't say to consider doing something like this "if" you have students with trauma. You have students with trauma. It's not "if" that trauma affects their ability to learn. It does. Establish that your classroom is a safe place for all students and give them tools and strategies to manage their emotions in healthy ways. Trauma can reveal itself as refusal to work, disrespect, pushback, impatience, noncompliance, withdrawal, disorganization, and even attention-seeking behaviors, the very kinds of behaviors we've addressed through the frustration busters so far. One way to minimize the potential for frustration in these areas is to establish class structures that address trauma (and stress, anxiety, etc.) in proactive ways.

Not only might *you* reclaim some joy, but your students probably will too.

Chapter 9

Setting Expectations and Building Routines

I HATE messy transitions. We all have teacher pet peeves, right? Well, one of mine is when I say to get a certain material out or open to a certain website and students start talking.

Wait, does getting a folder out require talking? Is your Chromebook voice activated?

Sarcasm aside, if messy transitions are a source of frustration to me, I probably need better routines and procedures.

Having clear, rehearsed, consistent routines and procedures helps our classes run smoothly with little direct intervention or effort from us. We often expect students to know what we mean. We tell them to be organized, to study, to turn in their homework, to pay attention, but unless we teach them *how* to do such things, many of them sincerely *don't* know. And even things they do know how to do, like sharpening a pencil, may be handled differently teacher to teacher, class to class. If we assume students know how we want it done but don't explicitly tell them, they'll have to guess, and may guess wrong. So many of the things that frustrate us can really be addressed by teaching our students how we want that thing done—and then following through consistently.

From how our students enter the room and what they do before the bell to what they should do if they forgot a pencil, need a tissue, or want to use the bathroom, procedures are the answer. How is homework turned in? When can a student sharpen their pencil? How are they dismissed from class?

Communicating Routines

Along with creating a culture of safety, respect, and trust in those early weeks, we are learning and practicing routines. I avoid standing at the front of the room and lecturing about these routines. Instead, I introduce them in a few ways.

First, in the "break in to sixth grade" activity we do on the first day of school, a number of the clues are about our class routines. As students solve these clues, they're also learning how things will work in our class.

Second, I post signage. Too much information posted on walls can be visually chaotic and even distracting. Instead, I select a few routines I think are important to have clearly delineated and post those around the room. My primary posted routines are how to ask to go to the bathroom (in my case, stand and hold up a sign language "r") and what I expect when I call for full attention.

In those early days, we practice. When you get ready to come to class, where will you find the list of what you need? (Posted by the door.) When you arrive, what should you do? (Join the Pear Deck and start our bell work.) How will Mrs. Powell call for our attention? (Slowly count down from five.) What will attention look like? (Hands still, voices off, eyes on the speaker.) Where should Chromebook bags be put? (Hang them off the back of our chair.) How are students dismissed? (Stay seated until Mrs. Powell dismisses you.)

When a routine or expectation starts to fall apart, no matter what time of year, we stop everything and rehearse it. A common weakness is how my third or fourth period block reenters the room after lunch. They come in jazzed up and seem to mistake our classroom for a gymnasium.

It's not.

So I have them all leave the room, and we practice entering the classroom in what we've defined as the "right" way.

These procedures will fall apart quickly if they're not followed consistently. But consistent application of these procedures will allow all these aspects of the day to flow easily and smoothly without the teacher having to manage it all. So much more energy, attention, and patience can be given to the actual *teaching* part of our job when we aren't also reminding students where to turn in their homework in February.

Preemptively Busting Frustration

In addition to classroom management procedures, I also love instructional procedures. I have a basic structure I follow for the vast majority of class days. This predictability feels safe for some students, especially students with executive functioning challenges. They can more successfully prepare for and navigate class because they know what will happen when, and what is needed for each step. This also lets us flow seamlessly from one lesson element to another. Remember those messy transitions I hate? There are fewer of those when students know exactly what it means to move from our retrieval practice to our mindfulness moment. Yes, variety is nice and has a place in all this. Suddenly changing it all up from time to time is exciting and can be very engaging. But for the average day, the predictability of routine provides some safety and smoothness for all of us.

A few of my favorite instructional routines are retrieval practice, mindfulness moments, and a lesson close. Each of these is broad enough to allow plenty of variety so that, even when these routines are used daily, our experience doesn't feel stale. They are based in the science of learning and leverage the way students' minds work to support long-term retention of our lesson content. Building these routines into my lesson planning helps me make sure I'm crafting lessons that make the best use of the time I get with my students.

Retrieval Practice

I first learned about retrieval practice in the book *Powerful Teaching* by Pooja K. Agarwal and Patrice M. Bain. One of my takeaways from their book is that it's perhaps less important how we teach content but more important what we have students *do* with that content. The book *Make It Stick* by Peter C. Brown, Henry L. Roediger III, and Mark A. McDaniel refers to retrieval practice as interrupting the process of forgetting. No matter how engaging and exciting our initial lesson was, students *will* start to forget it at some point. That content might still be in there somewhere, but students will lose the connections to it. By having them *retrieve* that content, we are keeping those connections strong and functional. After reading these books, retrieval practice became a set part of my bell work every day. I use a wide variety of retrieval activities, but the point is to have students pull up and use content so it stays "sticky."

Sometimes we use instructional software for retrieval practice. My students like Learning Farm, a site that lets them play ridiculous minigames after successfully answering questions. I am famously bad at Chicken Volleyball, so destroying Mrs. Powell seems to be an effective motivator. This is also a good place to use some of my favorite Lecture Busters, like Alphabet Soup and Junk Drawer.

It can also be appropriate to use a low-stakes quiz for retrieval practice, like Quizizz, Gimkit, or Kahoot!, or use flashcards (or a flashcard website like Quizlet). I often use software or one of the Lecture Busters for retrieval practice and then follow up with a quiz game maybe ten minutes later to encourage their brains to keep going back to that content so it really sticks. For more retrieval practice ideas, check out retrievalpractice.org, a site curated by Pooja K. Agarwal, one of the authors of the *Powerful Teaching* book.

Mindfulness Moments
....

After retrieval practice, we have what I've called a mindfulness moment. In truth, I'm using the term "mindfulness" perhaps too broadly for what I include in this time, but our purpose is to do something to encourage a positive brain state for learning. This is often described as "relaxed alertness." Achieving this state is not one-size-fits all. I didn't understand this at first. I diligently implemented brain breaks into my class after learning about them in some professional development, but after a *year* of using them, I was finding myself frustrated by how sometimes my students were so chaotic and wound up after them. Then I heard educational neuroscience expert Dr. Lori Desautels give a keynote at a conference, and she addressed this common problem by explaining that sometimes we need to wake the brain up, and sometimes we need to calm the nervous system down.

Oh.

So what my class needs first thing in the morning might not work for the class coming in right after lunch. To achieve that state of relaxed alertness, sometimes we need to wake students up. Sometimes we need to calm them down. Sometimes we need to address anxiety, fear, trauma, or just a downright bad start to the day. I take the time with our mindfulness moment to teach the student how the activity is good for their brain. They quickly buy in to this and seem to really like understanding what's happening in their brains and how to influence that. Here are some of my favorite mindfulness moment resources:

Brain Breaks

Our favorite energizing brain breaks get us moving.

This or That: My students like the This or That videos on YouTube. In these videos, students are directed to move to a side of the room to designate their choice between two items. Many of these videos then have them do a dance or exercise based on the side they chose.

The Greedy Game: We also like a game I first learned from the Everyday Mathematics series called the Greedy Game. We play a super simple version that goes like this: Every student stands up. I will roll a die. Their objective is to sit to lock in the sum total of all the numbers I've rolled and to be the last one to sit before I roll a 2. All students still standing when I roll a 2 get no points.

Stand If: One other one we like is called "Stand If." I pose a statement, like, "Stand if you like broccoli." Students stand if that's true for them. I usually mix up random questions and content questions to also review what we've been doing. This gets students moving and lets them share their interests, but does so in a way that is orderly and contained.

Exploring Feelings

Some mindfulness moments give students a chance to explore their own feelings. I *love* the templates Pear Deck has developed for this purpose. Sometimes I show students a list of feeling words and have them identify which they feel the most and explain why. Other similar activities show a series of memes and ask students which one they are today. You can ask students what made them happy today, or frustrated, or proud. When students can put words to what they're feeling, they can gain a sense of control over their emotions, and we have the opportunity to "check in" on their emotional well-being. Sometimes students are hurting and we don't see it. We can't assume that we would know. Instead, these kinds of activities, in a classroom of safety and respect, help us notice and understand what our students are feeling.

Calming Down

Sometimes we need calming. My favorite resources for this are the yoga exercises produced by ClassDojo and the Flow videos by GoNoodle. The ClassDojo yoga exercises are brief and very easy to do. Even if you don't use ClassDojo for points or any of their other features, you can still access these exercises in their Big Ideas section. They also have some great videos and exercises to help younger students identify and learn to deal with their emotions. The Flow videos from GoNoodle are designed to calm. They involve slowing breathing, relaxing the muscles, and learning to bring the body down from big feelings. My personal favorite is a video called "On/Off." This video is a focused relaxation exercise that I've noticed students applying on their own when they feel stressed or recognize they need to calm. Coloring is also very calming!

Using Humor

One other approach to preparing our brain for learning is humor. Laughter releases endorphins and serotonin, decreases cortisol (that stress hormone we first talked about in part 1), elevates mood, releases tension, and even temporarily boosts memory and attention. Don't we want *all* of that? We love playing brief, carefully previewed funny videos to get us laughing together. By the way, really cute videos, though they don't induce laughter, do have similar effects since the brain responds to "awww" very similarly to the way it responds to humor.

The Lesson Close

The final instructional routine I'd like to cover together is a strong lesson close. For whatever reason, before I read the book I mentioned earlier, *Powerful Teaching*, I'd developed a bad habit of stopping class wherever we ran out of time. Although it wasn't the first place I'd encountered this idea, one of the recommendations from the authors is to close lessons well. A strong closure reminds students what we've covered, prompts them to think about and organize what they've learned, and can even be an opportunity to collect data you can use to shape your instruction the next day.

Many of the same activities we'd use for retrieval practice can also be used to close a lesson well. I think of it like bookends—you know, the heavy things used to keep books from falling over on a shelf?

Typically a set of bookends are exactly the same, but one is turned the opposite way from the other to hold the books in place. Similarly, retrieval practice and the lesson close use very similar activities for different—but related—purposes. Retrieval practice is meant to pull up and strengthen the connections with what's been covered previously, whether yesterday or further back. We want students to call up what they've learned and use it. For a lesson close, we want students to identify what they've learned and organize their thinking. If the content of our lessons is like the books in this analogy, we need both retrieval practice and strong closure to keep the learning from falling over.

A lesson close is a great place to employ metacognition. Students identify what they know and what they don't know and reflect on how they learned. There are many great activities for self-reporting of mastery out there, activities such as having students use a red light, yellow light, or green light to identify how well they understood the topic. But to make this more powerful and effective, we need to partner this with a review of what we actually covered during class. Consider what happens if you ask a kid what they did at school today: "I don't know." Think of a strong lesson close like arming them with the answer to that question.

Another powerful aspect of a strong lesson close is supporting our students' organization. When I was just stopping the lesson wherever we were when the bell rang, I was often shouting any homework instructions or reminders over the chaos of students hurriedly packing up to leave my room.

I could basically just loop right back up to that frustration buster about missing homework, right? I was definitely NOT supporting my students' organization and was setting myself up for serious frustration later.

Instead, now I take a moment to remind them of what we've covered, then they do some kind of exit-ticket activity, and I remind them what they have for homework or what announcements they need to remember for tomorrow. This is *much* more organized, and the transition out of class is far calmer than it ever was before.

Retrieval practice, mindfulness moments, and a strong lesson close are three of the instructional routines I've leaned heavily on in recent years. Each is vetted by a wealth of research, and none takes more than a few minutes to do, making all three viable strategies for the vast majority of teaching settings.

Just for fun, I'll end this chapter with a lesson close:

We covered procedural and instructional routines that prevent frustration by allowing class to run smoothly and effectively. We looked at how to establish these routines, what to do when they fall apart, and the benefit of routine to students. I provided samples of some of my favorite instructional routines and referred to some other resources to find more.

You have no homework tonight. You're an adult (probably?). I don't know, go enjoy a beverage, take a walk, snuggle someone you love, or put on your favorite pair of fuzzy socks. Sound good?

To reflect on what we've covered, let's try an activity called Junk Drawer.

How does this image relate to this chapter?

Curious about this . . . weird . . . activity? We'll talk about Junk Drawer in more depth in chapter 11.

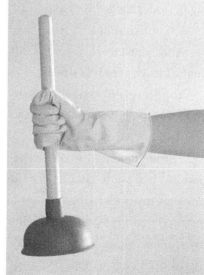

Chapter 10

GAMIFICATION

I'm going to tell you something you may find hard to believe. But I promise you, it's true. And it's not because of anything about me at all. It's all thanks to the power of gamification.

Most of my students are independently motivated. They line up, begging to retake skills to demonstrate mastery. Even when the grading period is long closed and I can't change their grade.

I'm not kidding.

And I don't teach at some school for independently motivated students. I teach *very* real students.

You see, gamification is a system that creates a sense of motivation and drive to demonstrate mastery that is, well, kind of amazing.

And not hard at all to do.

Throughout this book, we've covered many classroom frustrations. When we looked at my functional frustration assessment, we saw that my underlying feelings are that I'm frustrated at the loss of instructional time and that I wind up feeling like a bad teacher, that my students should *want* to participate better. It's sincerely challenging to keep engagement levels up so high that our students *want* to participate all the time. Even when individual lessons and activities are highly engaging, it can be hard to sustain that level of engagement throughout all of our class structures every day. For me, gamification has been magic. It has been that underlying structure behind everything we do in class that ties it all together, makes it all meaningful, and fosters buy-in for the vast majority of my students.

A few years ago, I read *Explore Like a Pirate* by Michael Matera. As I read, I recognized my students in the descriptions of the different kinds of gamers. I do not consider myself a gamer, though I grew up with Mario and Sonic and have been known to lose miserably to my kids in Super Smash Bros. In fact, if you ask them what my special move is, it's what they call "the mom"—falling straight off the edge of the map. But I knew my students would really respond to the idea of gamification in our class.

What Is Gamification?

In a broad sense, gamification is bringing elements of video gaming into the classroom. This isn't exactly *playing* games. Sure, that can be part of it. But gamification looks at motivation and engagement. Researchers considered why kids would willingly play a game for hours on end—or more—even though they were failing over and over again, yet balk and give up the moment things got difficult at school. This led to an understanding of how elements of gaming can be leveraged for powerful learning. In a video game, a player can make choices, earn customizations, compete or collaborate with others, see their progress, and, well, win. Gamification in education has grown into a very wide concept, and there are tons of great educators out there doing it well. Check out #xlap on Twitter to connect with more people and ideas around gamification in education.

Badging

I liked the idea of badging—that is, as my students demonstrated mastery of a standard or skill, they could earn a badge, hopefully motivating them to collect them and keep mastering content. But, I also knew I struggle with organization and would have a tough time keeping up with it. So, after some trial and error, I settled on a system we've used ever since.

And we *love* it.

To track progress, we use punch cards, like the loyalty rewards cards some stores use, where you get a punch every time you buy a sandwich. One card is for conduct and one is for content. The conduct cards are tied to ClassDojo. I award points for winning review games, showing extraordinary character, and meeting some basic expectations. ClassDojo lets us easily keep track of those points, and students can even redeem points right in the app now. Students can earn a card for every thirty points earned and redeem that card for a reward or save it toward more "expensive" rewards.

On the content card, I put skills or concepts I expect students to master during that unit. When we assess a skill or concept, students who demonstrate mastery (typically 80 percent or higher) get that skill punched on their content card.

I allow relearning and retakes, so even if we move on as a class, students can continue to work toward a punch on an "old" skill, even on previous cards (and, yes, students independently ask me to work with them on skills from *weeks* ago if they don't have it punched and are working toward a special reward). I've talked before about the importance of feedback and revisions. This is where we really see the magic in our gamification system. Students have a tangible, concrete record of what they've mastered and what they haven't, and this helps them set goals and track progress. With small-group remediation and one-on-one lessons, students refine their understanding of a skill and try again. And again, if needed. If the way I originally assessed the skill isn't working for a student, we can try something else. The point is that they demonstrate mastery, not *how* they demonstrate that mastery.

When we start a new unit, I create and print a new content mission card, but students can continue working on old cards. We use some of our advisory period, and I send students resources they can review independently to prepare for retakes of older material. Sometimes I also reserve portions of class to go back over a skill I notice multiple students have not yet mastered. A completed card can be redeemed for rewards, just like the conduct cards. Completed content cards and conduct cards have the same value and can be used together toward higher-level rewards.

Students are responsible for keeping their cards and bringing them to class. I don't make a big deal over it if they forget them, but I typically won't let students go to their locker to retrieve forgotten cards. My thought is that a bit of reward for being organized and motivated enough to actually *have* them in class is OK! But if a student brings their forgotten cards another day, I'll happily catch them up with the punches they missed. After all, like we've discussed with missing supplies and other organizational needs, there are plenty of reasons a student (or any human being) might forget things from time to time, so exercising grace and tagging in some of those same strategies are still important here.

I have tried digital versions of the card system and turning the mission cards into "quests," and though there are many educators who do that very well, my students and I found it made their progress less tangible—there's something about holding the card in their hand, seeing the punched skills and unpunched skills, that makes their progress feel much more concrete.

Power-Up Rewards

Our power-up reward system is leveled. Basic rewards are level 1, meaning students need to turn in one card to claim one of those rewards. Some are tangible rewards, like something from our treasure chest, and others are customizations, like the right to use a small fidget in class. There are also nonitem rewards, like earning a happy phone call to their families.

The higher the reward level, the more cards necessary to redeem those rewards. Some of these rewards also require a bit more responsibility from the students, but I have reasonable confidence that a student who can "afford" a reward like that has already demonstrated strong effort and conduct. Customizations to their class experience have included choosing their own seat, getting to listen to their own music during class, the ability to eat a snack in class every day, and even getting to use slime in class (as I mentioned earlier in the Fads section of chapter 5). If students are "into" something, we add it. There's even a power-up that lets them create their own reward.

To engage and motivate my students who are driven by competition, my classes compete in what we call the Golden Squirrel competition. Seriously, the trophy is possession of a squirrel stuffed animal I spray-painted gold. Every few weeks, I see how many ClassDojo points each class has, and whichever class has more (averaged to account for differences in class size if needed) earns a temporary whole-class reward. To boost their class's score or lower the other class's, students can choose power-ups to protect themselves or "attack" another class. This is *very* motivating for some students, and they'll develop elaborate strategies and get other students on board to "purchase" and use power-ups in tandem.

Now, one note: I don't allow students to pool cards. I think that would offer an "out" to a student who otherwise needs to be motivated to dig in and try hard. If another student could just rescue them, why would that student need to work hard himself?

Building Extrinsic Motivation

After reading about my system, you may be tempted to think my adaptation of gamification centers around extrinsic motivation. Let me ask you something, though: Have you ever found an extrinsic motivation system that continues to work—well—long-term? The reality is that extrinsic motivators only work for a finite time. At some point, we need to move the motivation from extrinsic to intrinsic.

And this system does that beautifully.

You may have missed it. Remember how students get punches for mastering content? Remember how if a student isn't at mastery, they work hard and try again and can earn punches on old content, no matter how long ago we covered it? That's where the magic happens. Each year, it takes a while for this to build. At first, kids are kind of motivated by earning a prize or the right to have snacks in class, but the excitement level isn't extraordinary or anything. But then, usually a couple months in, around the time we move on to our second content card, students start to see their classmates earning higher-level customizations, and they start to want those too. They bring me their cards, and we look at the unpunched skills. Usually there's just one or two left by the time we've moved on in class. The student will say, "What can I do to get this skill punched?" Then we sit down together and go over the skill, and I assess them. And they get it.

I punch their card. Or, better yet, I hand their card back for *them* to punch.

And they look at me. Usually they blink for a beat or two.

And then a grin spreads across their face in slow motion.

"I did it?"

"Yes, yes you did! *You* did it!"

Some students, especially those we classically consider hard to motivate, aren't accustomed to feeling this kind of success. I assure you, the magic isn't in earning a snack or a pot of slime. The magic is in this moment, the moment they took on something hard and mastered it. Once they feel it, they're hooked. This gamification system takes something intangible, like effort or progress, and makes it tangible. The student can see it, hold it. They get it.

And they want more.

What makes this system work isn't that students get a reward. It's that they realize what it feels like to work hard and accomplish something. The extrinsic reward might be the carrot they're originally working toward, but that feeling of accomplishment is what they'll keep chasing.

Since implementing this system, I don't have to hound kids to get them try harder or improve their grades. I don't have to lecture on the importance of mastering every skill. They get it.

Now, OK, so sometimes a kid loses their cards and acts like they don't care. But then I have to reconsider what their leverage point may be and how to reengage them. Or maybe they've fallen behind in mastery and are discouraged by how hard it would be to catch up, so they need a little coaching. The cards are *not* meant to be punitive. This is a celebration of mastery and a tangible way to understand their progress. Do I really get 100 percent engagement and 100 percent mastery 100 percent of the time? Maybe not. But, seriously, it's pretty doggone close. And just think of how many potential frustrations I'm cutting off at the pass!

This shift to gamification has been very powerful, but it's also sincerely really easy. All I'm doing is basically printing my learning targets on a card for each student, grading select formative assessments I'd already be grading, and then punching their cards so they can see their progress and take ownership of their development of mastery. Logistically, it's very simple. These mission cards don't require an overhaul in how you teach. There's no program to download. Nothing to learn to do. You're just making their learning visible. That's it.

But my, is it powerful.

Additional Resources

If you're interested in finding out more about gamification and the many, many different ways educators all over the world are applying it in their own classes, I encourage you to check out the following resources:

- *Explore Like a Pirate* by Michael Matera

- Michael's website, MrMatera.com
- #xlap on Twitter

Since gamification really began to gain traction in 2010, there have been dozens of books published on the topic.[1] Because I haven't read them, I'm not comfortable offering any other specific recommendations here, but I will say that if this is a pool you want to jump into, you can swim for quite a while!

Chapter 11

Boredom Busters

Throughout this book, I've referenced several activities from my previous book, *Boredom Busters*. If you're already familiar with those activities or that book, great! If not, I want to offer a bit more information about them.

Boredom Busters are low- or no-prep, low- or no-materials activities that leverage curiosity and novelty to increase buy-in, engagement, and depth. They are designed to work with any content, any grade level, any educational setting. In *Boredom Busters* and on my website, I offer three kinds of "Buster" activities: Worksheet Busters, Lecture Busters, and Homework Busters.

These busters were born out of a desire to respect teachers' already limited time and money while offering creative ways to better engage our students in typically low-engagement activities (worksheets, lectures, and going over homework).

Want to find out more about the activities that follow or any of my other Boredom Busters? Check out teachbeyondthedesk.com, and as with anything else in this book, please reach out with questions: @beyond_the_desk. I sincerely believe we are all in this together and that the community of educators supporting one another is a beautiful, powerful thing. It's an honor to be part of that. So reach out, share what you're up to, and let's be part of that wonderful community together.

Worksheet Busters

Worksheet Busters are novel, highly engaging ways to deploy a worksheet. Instead of just answering the question on the page, students might be flying Paper Airplanes, playing Musical Desks, or even going Speed Dating.

Below are the Worksheet Busters I referenced in this book: Paper Airplanes and Hungry Hippos.

Hungry Hippos

There are multiple variations of Hungry Hippos, but here I've outlined the one I use as a back-to-school activity:

Materials:

For this Worksheet Buster, you'll need a set of plastic ball pit balls and a printed list of back-to-school discussion prompts. These may relate to what students did over the summer, their personal interests, your class routines, or anything else you think will allow them to get to know each other, get to know you, and for you to get to know them.

Setup:

Cut apart the question set or worksheet and tape one question on each ball. Note: if you're new to my ideas, you may not know this, but the word "ball" is risky with some audiences, so I call these "learning spheres." You're welcome.

Gameplay

1. At your signal, each player rushes to the pile of balls (or learning spheres) and selects one.

2. Arrange students in groups, such as by the color of ball they selected. Each student reads their question, and then everyone in the group answers that question.

3. The benefits of covering the questions this way versus just having students read and answer their own questions are that students get to share more of their own thoughts and that they aren't "done" once they've read their own question. Wait time quickly leads to off-task behavior, so this approach keeps students engaged.

4. While students discuss, I join each group for a few minutes at a time, asking for more information, sharing some of my own thoughts, and listening attentively for some of the really helpful info I know I've loaded into some of these questions.

5. At the end of the round, students return their ball and select another one.

To keep the activity moving and solicit some feedback on learning I can use to drive the rest of the lesson, I also like to draw a few questions to discuss as a whole group between rounds. Students can even share a great answer they heard from someone else in their group. I like to have students share others group members' answers because it encourages good listening and valuing others' thoughts instead of focusing only on their own.

This is my list of back-to-school Hungry Hippos questions. It's my no means exhaustive, so tweak, revise, and add your own!

- Describe your biggest adventure this summer.
- What was your favorite place you went this summer?
- What is your favorite thing about summer?
- Who did you miss most over the summer?
- What will you miss most about summer?
- Describe your favorite day of summer break.
- What's one thing you didn't get to do this summer that you really wanted to do?

- Who did you spend the most time with over the summer?
- What is something you learned or learned to do better this summer?
- What is your biggest regret of the summer?
- What are you looking forward to most about this year?
- Are you feeling more nervous or excited about this year?
- What is your favorite thing about ___ grade so far?
- Do you think you'll like this class? Explain.
- What's something you're curious about for this year?
- What's something you'll miss about _____ grade?
- What was your favorite thing about _____ grade?
- Who has been your favorite teacher so far? Why?
- What makes a teacher a "good" teacher?
- What makes a teacher a "bad" teacher?
- What are you most proud of?
- What are you good at?
- What do you like least about school?
- What sports or activities do you enjoy?
- What makes a book a good book? What makes a book a bad book?
- Do you like writing better when you're told what to write or when it's left up to you?
- Do you think you're a good writer? Explain.
- Do you think you're a good reader? Explain.
- What do you wish teachers understood?
- What do you wish parents/guardians understood?

Paper Airplanes

Materials:

For this buster, all you need is a worksheet for each student.

Setup:

Students put their names on their worksheet and do the first problem.

Gameplay:

1. After finishing the first problem, students fold their worksheet into an airplane.

2. Students stand and hold their paper airplanes. At your signal, they throw their airplane toward the other side or the middle of the room. Note: make it clear their airplanes do not leave their fingers until you tell them to do so.

3. Each students grabs the nearest worksheet and does one more problem, initialing every problem they do throughout the rest of the game.

   Students who find extra airplanes should hold them high in the air, so others who are still looking can easily find them. Although teachers fear the loss of time, I've used Paper Airplanes in rooms of hundreds of educators, and we've found all the airplanes and returned to our seats in minutes. Kids are excellent at looking under desks and tracking down rene-gade projectiles.

4. Repeat steps one through three until the end of playing time or until the worksheets are finished.

5. Students get their original worksheet back and evaluate all the answers contributed on it. Have them leave the original answer but mark any corrections below or beside it. This allows you to track students' understanding across the worksheets. Make it clear that students will be graded on what they submit on their worksheet, so it is up to them to catch and correct mistakes.

Lecture Busters

Lecture Busters are checks for understanding that require students to construct meaning from your content and retrieve their learning in novel ways. These activities are a great way to break up lectures or close a lesson. The Lecture Busters referenced in this book are Alphabet Soup and Junk Drawer, which I explain below.

Alphabet Soup

For Alphabet Soup, teachers indicate a letter of the alphabet, and students identify a term or idea that starts with that letter and relates to the lesson content. There are two main variations: You can have all students do the same letter or let each student draw their own letter. Discussing what they came up with provides an effective review of the content and provides you with some feedback about what they understood (and what, perhaps, they didn't).

Materials:

Alphabet cards or random letter picker

Setup:

Draw one letter for the whole class to consider and give students a couple minutes to turn and talk to each other.

Gameplay:

1. Each student comes up with a term that starts with the letter you drew and that is relevant to the material you've just covered.
2. After a few minutes, stop their discussion and let turn-and-talk pairs share aloud.

Once a term has been shared, it cannot be repeated, forcing remaining partnerships to think deeper. The advantage of this approach is that, by the whole class using the same letter, you're able to compare and discuss the various interpretations of the same idea. You can see which terms and ideas are the easiest for students to come up with, which concepts are coming up most often, and what novel ideas are generated when students are forced to think again to come up with a term that hasn't already been shared.

Variation:

Instead of using the same letter for the whole class, each partnership draws their own letter and follows the same routine outlined above.

The advantage to this approach is that some students benefit from the small act of selecting their own item, and then you get to discuss a wide variety of ideas revealed by the diversity of letters in play. However, you don't quite get the stark comparison explained above that happens when so many people get to interpret the same letter.

Junk Drawer

Similarly, for Junk Drawer, you give students an image, like a plunger, and ask them how that relates to your recent content. Typically the connection is not something they can find in their notes or textbook, so they are having to think outside the box to make and describe their own connections. The novelty is engaging, and the results are both insightful and fun.

Junk Drawer also has two ways to play:

Materials:
Junk Drawer cards, available as a printout on teachbeyondthedesk.com, or other random item images.

Setup:
Select an object for the whole class to consider.

Gameplay:

1. Give students a couple minutes to turn and talk about it. They should think of a relevant way to connect it to what you've just covered.
2. After a few minutes, stop their discussions and let turn-and-talk pairs share aloud.

The advantage of this approach is that by using the same item for the whole class, you are able to compare and discuss together the various interpretations of that shared item.

Variation:

Assign different items for each student or partnership and follow the same routine. The advantage to this approach is that some students benefit from the small act of selecting their own item, and you get to discuss a wide variety of ideas and concepts. However, you don't quite get the stark comparison that happens when so many people get to interpret the same item.

Homework Busters

Homework Busters are designed to make grading more efficient, drive the assignment deeper, provide useful feedback, and/or extend the learning beyond the grade. The Homework Busters I've referenced earlier in this book are Error Analysis and Homework Quizzes.

Error Analysis

When we go over assignments or grade them, students see the grade as an indication that the assignment is "done," and it probably lands in a recycle bin, backpack, or locker. But we don't want the learning to stop just because the assignment is graded. We want students to think about *why* they got a problem right or wrong. We want them to learn from their mistakes. Error Analysis is one way to guide students to analyze their work. After checking an assignment, students complete an Error Analysis form to analyze their own work.

Name_____Assignment_____

Homework Error Analysis

Problem #	✓ or X	Explain your error	Justify/prove the correct answer	What will you do differently next time?

The printable version of this form is available
on teachbeyondthedesk.com.

Homework Quizzes

The day a homework assignment is due, instead of collecting or grading the assignment, give a brief quiz with questions over the assignment. I tend to select five questions from the assignment, or three from the assignment with two that use the same skill but have unique content. Five questions are far easier to grade than an entire assignment. You don't have to fuss over getting assignments turned in and tracking down late work, because every student who is present participates. This frees you from the typical homework headaches. The quiz itself and its score holds students accountable for doing the work.

Conclusion

We Can't Afford to Lose You

7.3 billion dollars a year.

It can be hard to get people outside the world of education—or sometimes, unfortunately, high up in education—to care about issues affecting teachers.

But 7.3 *billion* dollars. That's only the financial cost, remember, of teacher burnout and turnover. We *have* to care about this. We can't afford not to.

Statistically, if a district hires ten teachers, six of those are to replace retiring teachers. That means 40 percent of annual hires are replacing teachers who left the profession for other reasons.

Some of those reasons are fine. Teachers move. Maybe they took a different position in education. Maybe they're stepping out for family reasons.

But 43 percent of those who left before retirement didn't. They left due to stress.

With enrollment in teacher preparation programs dropping by a third over the last ten years, it's getting harder and harder to fill those vacancies.

Will there come a day when there *are* no teachers left to hire?

I hope not. I love our profession. We need to save it.

Teachers, if you are reading this, I see you. I see how hard you work. I see how exhausted you are. I see how you feel like you're not enough. And I see how much you still love it when you get those lightbulb moments with your students or when they put a tissue on their head and rename themself George. (That might be a story for another day.)

Teachers, we *have* to support each other. We need to let each other teach differently, handle issues differently, plan differently, communicate differently, *be* different. There is not one right way to do this job well. We can't afford to be cutting each other down and fighting among ourselves.

We are under attack. When test scores aren't high enough, pay too low, class sizes too large, we receive the bulk of the blame with little respect as professionals to have a voice in what really needs to happen next in our field. We have to stand together. Let's leave no man behind. Let's link shields and form a testudo, a giant shell to cover us all so we can move forward—together—protected from any adversary, including the stress within.

We have to notice each other. No teacher should go through their day alone, isolated, lonely. Let's pop open the bag of reward candy and lesson-plan together over a few Twix bars and some shared laughter and tears.

We have to do a better job supporting new hires. We can't keep losing them like this. We can't keep losing *us* like this.

Principals, if you are reading this, we *desperately* need your help.

Do you know the top stressor teachers name as the reason they leave the profession early?

Lack of support from their principals.

Look, I see how much is on your plate. I see how many requirements are pushed down on you from above that you have no real control over. I see that you are responsible for leading the school climate for your students and the working conditions for your staff while busting up fights, running staff meetings, making sure the gym is unlocked for that after-school club, satisfying upset parents, and making sure all your compulsory paperwork is turned in to the administration above you. And standardized testing.

I don't envy you. But we need you.

Please, give us a voice.

And then listen to what we say.

There's still so much capacity for joy in what we do. I want you to take a minute. Look at your class list. Pull up some photos. Open your happy file of sweet notes and drawings from students over the years. Think about the time Avery drew you as Ms. Frizzle or your students made an epic zombie movie to warn against the dangers of addiction to technology. Think about lunches spent with kids, them teaching you the newest memes and how to use "drip" appropriately. Think about how Colton decided constructed responses were a game he was going to win and then obsessed over getting a higher score than anyone else, eventually moving himself from below average to above average on the standardized test. Take a look at the jar of sweet notes Alivia and her mom arranged to thank you for supporting them through a par-ticularly tough year. Read that note from Sydney when she graduated a semester early and wanted to thank you for helping her through her junior high years.

Look through your lesson plans. What's that project or unit you *love*, that you get giddily excited over? Mine's Percy Jackson. We dis-cover we have magical abilities and become demigod campers at Camp Half-Blood. We write our own epic quest stories and celebrate just how far we've come in a year. Percy finishes his year at Camp Half-Blood with a letter from his mom, so my students finish their year with a letter from their parents and families, expressing how proud of them they are, for all they've accomplished and all they are.

We all cry.

I'm crying now writing about it.

These are the happy tears.

Have you found a bit of the joy?

I know I don't have all the answers. But you know, I think we can figure it out together.

I'd like to close with an activity I learned from Gail Heinemeyer, faculty member of the Leadership Institute of the Association for Middle Level Education. At the conclusion of the Institute, after days of learning together, participants are asked what they will stand for, *who* they will stand for.

They think of the student or teacher who needs more of their attention, and they commit to stand for that person in the coming year.

I ask you, who will you stand for?

I stand for you.

Sincerely,
Katie

Endnotes

Chapter 1

1   Diane Stark Rentner et al., *Listen to Us: Teacher Views and Voices*,
    Center on Education Policy, May 2016, 4, eric.ed.gov/?q=Listen+to
    +Us%3a+Teacher+Views+and+Voices&id=ED568172.

2   Borderless Charity, "The Impact of Teacher Burnout and What We
    Can Do Abou t It," Medium, March 30, 2018, medium.com/
    @TheCharity/the-impact-of-teacher-burnout-and-what-we-can
    -do-about-it-4ffadd64417c.

3   Matthew Ronfeldt et al., *How Teacher Turnover Harms Student
    Achievement*, Calder Center, January 2012, pages 13-23.
    caldercenter.org/sites/default/files/Ronfeldt-et-al.pdf.

4   Kassondra Grenata, "Teacher Stress and Disengagement Impacts
    Student Performance," Education World, 2014, educationworld
    .com/a_curr/teacher-stress-impacts-student-performance.shtml.

5   University of British Columbia, "Stress Contagion Possible
    Amongst Students, Teachers," Science Daily, June 27, 2016,
    sciencedaily.com/releases/2016/06/160627124928.htm.

6   Sarah D. Sparks, "How Teachers' Stress Affects Students: A
    Research Roundup," *Education Week*, June 7, 2017, edweek.org/
    tm/articles/2017/06/07/how-teachers-stress-affects-students-a
    -research.html?print=1.

7   Andrea Bonior, "'Frustrated?' There's Probably Another Emotion
    Present," *Psychology Today*, September 27, 2019, psychologytoday
    .com/us/blog/friendship-20/201909/frustrated-theres-probably
    -another-emotion-present.

Chapter 2

1 Catherine Gewertz, "Teacher Praise Helps Students Focus, Behave Better, Study Says," *Education Week*, January 30, 2020, edweek.org/teaching-learning/teacher-praise-helps-students-focus-behave-better-study-says/2020/01.

2 Sarah D. Sparks, "Getting Feedback Right: A Q&A With John Hattie," *Education Week*, June 19, 2018, edweek.org/leadership/getting-feedback-right-a-q-a-with-john-hattie/2018/06.

3 Thomas R. Guskey, "Grades versus Comments: Research on Student Feedback," Kappan Online, October 28, 2019, kappanonline.org/grades-versus-comments-research-student-feedback-guskey/.

4 Heather Voke, "Motivating Students to Learn," *ASCD Infobrief* 2 (28), 2002.

5 Katie Powell, *Boredom Busters: Transform Worksheets, Lectures, and Grading into Engaging, Meaningful Learning*, San Diego, CA: Dave Burgess Consulting Inc., 2019.

6 Susan M. Sheridan, "Establishing Healthy Parent-Teacher Relationships for Early Learning Success," *Early Learning Network*, August 29, 2018, earlylearningnetwork.unl.edu/2018/08/29/parent-teacher-relationships/.

Chapter 5

1 Sarah D. Sparks, "Why Teacher-Student Relationships Matter," *Education Week*, March 12 2019, edweek.org/teaching-learning/why-teacher-student-relationships-matter/2019/03.

2 Carol Ann Tomlinson, "One to Grow On: Respecting Students," ASCD, September 1, 2011, ascd.org/el/articles/respecting-students.

3 Sarah D. Sparks, "How Feeling Respected Transforms a Student's Relationship to School," PBS, August 4, 2016, pbs.org/newshour/education/feeling-respected-transforms-student-school.

4 Becky A. Bailey, *Conscious Discipline: Building Resilient Schools and Homes* (Oviedo, FL: Loving Guidance, 2019), sendat.academy/

wp-content/uploads/2020/12/eCD-Participant-Guide-Complete
.pdf.

Chapter 7

1   Meera Jagannathan, "Teachers Were Already Leaving the
Profession Due to Stress—Then COVID-19 Hit," *MarketWatch*,
March 1, 2021, marketwatch.com/story/teachers-were-already
-leaving-the-profession-due-to-stress-then-covid-19-hit
-11614025213.

Chapter 10

1   Christo Dichev and Darina Dicheva, "Gamifying Education:
What is Known, What is Believed, and What Remains Uncertain:
A Critical Review," *Educational Technology Journal*, February
20, 2017, educationaltechnologyjournal.springeropen.com/
articles/10.1186/s41239-017-0042-5.

References

Agarwal, P. K., and P. M. Bain. *Powerful Teaching: Unleash the Science of Learning.* San Francisco, CA: Jossey-Bass, 2019.

American Federation of Teachers. *Educator Quality of Work Life Survey.* Washington, DC: American Federation of Teachers, 2017. aft.org/sites/default/files/2017_eqwl_survey_web.pdf.

Bailey, Becky A. *Conscious Discipline: Building Resilient Schools and Homes.* Oviedo, FL: Loving Guidance, 2019. sendat.academy/wp-content/uploads/2020/12/eCD-Participant-Guide-Complete.pdf.

Bonior, Andrea. "Frustrated?' There's Probably Another Emotion Present." *Psychology Today.* September 27, 2019. psychologytoday.com/us/blog/friendship-20/201909/frustrated-theres-probably-another-emotion-present.

Borderless Charity. "The Impact of Teacher Burnout and What We Can Do About It." Medium. March 30, 2018. medium.com/@TheCharity/the-impact-of-teacher-burnout-and-what-we-can-do-about-it-4ffadd64417c.

Brown, Peter C. *Make It Stick: The Science of Successful Learning.* Cambridge, MA: Belknap Press, 2014.

Dichey, Christo, and Darina Dicheva. "Gamifying Education: What is Known, What is Believed and What Remains Uncertain: A Critical Review." *Educational Technology Journal,* 2017. educationaltechnologyjournal.springeropen.com/articles/10.1186/s41239-017-0042-5.

Dweck, C. S. *Mindset: Changing the Way You Think to Fulfill Your Potential.* London: Robinson, 2017.

Gewertz, Catherine. "Teacher Praise Helps Students Focus, Behave Better, Study Says." *Education Week,* January 30, 2020. edweek.

org/teaching-learning/teacher-praise-helps -students-focus-behave-better-study-says/2020/01.

Granata, Kassondra. "Teacher Stress and Disengagement Impacts Student Performance." *Education World*. 2014. educationworld. com/a_curr/teacher-stress-impacts-student-performance.shtml.

Guskey, Thomas R. "Grades versus Comments: Research on Student Feedback." Kappan Online. October 28, 2019. kappanonline.org/ grades-versus-comments-research-student-feedback-guskey/.

Jagannathan, Meera. "Teachers Were Already Leaving the Profession Due to Stress—Then COVID-19 Hit." *MarketWatch*, March 1, 2021. marketwatch.com/story/teachers-were-already-leaving-the -profession-due-to-stress-then-covid-19-hit-11614025213.

Matera, Michael. *Explore Like a Pirate: Gamification and Game-Inspired Course Design to Engage, Enrich, and Elevate Your Learners*. San Diego, CA: Dave Burgess Consulting, 2015.

Matera, Michael, and John Meehan. *Fully Engaged: Playful Pedagogy for Real Results*. San Diego, CA: Dave Burgess Consulting, 2021.

Meehan, John. *EDrenaline Rush: Game-Changing Student Engagement Inspired by Theme Parks, Mud Runs, and Escape Rooms*. San Diego, CA: Dave Burgess Consulting, 2019.

Miller, Matt. *Ditch That Textbook: Free Your Teaching and Revolutionize Your Classroom*. San Diego, CA: Dave Burgess Consulting, 2015.

Powell, Katie. *Boredom Busters: Transform Worksheets, Lectures, and Grading into Engaging, Meaningful Learning Experiences*. San Diego, CA: Dave Burgess Consulting, 2019.

Rentner, Diane Stark, et al. *Listen to Us: Teacher Views and Voices*. Institute of Education Sciences. May 2016. files.eric.ed.gov/ fulltext/ED568172.pdf.

Ronfeldt, Matthew, et al. *How Teacher Turnover Harms Student Achievement*. Calder Center. January 2012. caldercenter.org/sites/ default/files/Ronfeldt-et-al.pdf.

Sheridan, Susan M. "Establishing Healthy Parent-Teacher Relationships for Early Learning Success." *Early Learning Network*. August 29, 2018. earlylearningnetwork.unl. edu/2018/08/29/parent-teacher-relationships/.

Sparks, Sarah D. "Getting Feedback Right: A Q&A With John Hattie." *Education Week*. June 19, 2018. edweek.org/leadership/ getting-feedback-right-a-q-a-with-john-hattie/2018/06.

Sparks, Sarah D. "How Feeling Respected Transforms a Student's Relationship to School." *NewsHour*. August 4, 2016. pbs.org/ newshour/education/feeling-respected-transforms -student-school.

Sparks, Sarah D. "How Teachers' Stress Affects Students: A Research Roundup." *Education Week*. June 7, 2017. edweek.org/tm/ articles/2017/06/07/how-teachers-stress-affects-students-a -research.html?print=1.

Sparks, Sarah D. "Why Teacher-Student Relationships Matter." *Education Week*. March 12, 2019. edweek.org/teaching-learning/ why-teacher-student-relationships-matter/2019/03.

Tomlinson, Carol Ann. "One to Grow On: Respecting Students." ASCD. September 1, 2011. www.ascd.org/el/articles/ respecting-students.

University of British Columbia. "Stress Contagion Possible Amongst Students, Teachers." *Science Daily*. June 27, 2016. sciencedaily .com/releases/2016/06/160627124928.htm.

Wright, Jim. "Engaging the Student as an Active RTI Partner in the Intervention Planning Process." Intervention Central. 2010. interventioncentral.org/sites/default/files/rti_student _engagement.pdf.

Voke, Heather. "Motivating Students to Learn." *ASCD Infobrief* 2 (28), 2002.

Acknowledgements

The acknowledgements in my first book, *Boredom Busters*, was my attempt at generating a thorough list of all those who made that work possible. It lists my childhood teachers, colleagues from the early years of my career, mentors, friends, and family. In the years between the publication of that book and this one, that list has continued to grow.

In 2019, due to some challenging family circumstances, my family moved out of our home and moved in with friends. When *Boredom Busters* was released, I was technically homeless, since living in another family's home qualified my children for homeless student assistance. I unboxed the first copies of the book from my friend's couch, since my own was in storage in their garage.

Sometimes life is hard.

But when so much in my life seemed uncertain—and even unfair—I discovered that I was truly rich. No, it wasn't about money. Y'all, I was a homeless teacher. You *know* I wasn't rich in the traditional sense! Instead, I discovered that I was rich in relationships. People. Friends.

To the people who showed me love in such tangible ways, who loved my family, who carried us through some of our hardest days: thank you.

I posted a blog and video for New Years in 2020 reflecting on everything my family had walked through in 2019. I looked into the camera, tears in my eyes, and said that nothing 2020 would bring could be as hard as 2019.

And then a pandemic struck.

I don't mean to minimize the harsh, heartbreaking reality of the pandemic and the COVID-19 virus, but, y'all, 2020 was still easier for my family than 2019. We quarantined in our own home, having moved there in November 2019. We spent days on end in pajamas, eating our body weight in snacks, having groceries delivered, all of us working and learning from home, together. After the hardship of our 2019, that time together was, in many ways, a blessing.

But the continued effects of the pandemic on the world, particularly the field of education, cannot be minimized. This is hard. And even beyond the consequences of the pandemic, many in our profession are struggling. As we've covered in this book, we are losing quality teachers at an alarming rate, and the number of preservice teachers moving into the field seems too low to keep up.

Perhaps this isn't the way "acknowledgments" typically read. I'm OK with that. As I write this, schools are struggling to find coverage for quarantined teachers, students are stealing soap dispensers off school bathroom walls in a baffling TikTok trend, teachers are covering extra duties on their prep periods to try to fill in where subs are unavailable, and it seems like everyone's pretty tired. Exhausted. Despondent? Maybe. So, yeah, these acknowledgments are a bit unusual. These are unusual times. And I'm the author! I guess that gives me the authority to do weird things with my book if I want to.

So my acknowledgments acknowledge that life can be hard, that we need each other, and that I hope we can eventually turn this ship toward smoother seas.

On my hardest days, I know I wouldn't have made it through without those stellar people in my world. From tech tips to text chains during Zoom staff meetings, packages of treats dropped off on porches to prayers shared earnestly, I saw again how we are so much better together. I am rich in friends.

If you are reading this today and your circle of people feels too small or incomplete—or perhaps nonexistent—please reach out. Not only is our profession too hard to do alone, but so is life. If your circle is too small, let me join it. I'll bring some friends. Not only will your circle grow, mine will too. And the next time life throws some new challenge our way, we'll be ready.

Let's lean in, stand together, and take good care of each other.

About Katie Powell

Katie Powell is the director for middle level programs for the Association for Middle Level Education. She began teaching in 2005 and has served as a special education teacher, Title I teacher, instructional coach, and classroom teacher. Katie's first book, *Boredom Busters,* grew out of this focus on providing interventions for struggling students by leveraging curiosity and fun to increase engagement while driving learning deeper. Katie believes in respecting the expertise of teachers and shares her creative process so they can address instruction and classroom management within their own teaching styles.

Connect with Katie on Twitter @beyond_the_desk.

MORE FROM
DAVE BURGESS
Consulting, Inc.

Since 2012, DBCI has published books that inspire and equip educators to be their best. For more information on our titles or to purchase bulk orders for your school, district, or book study, visit **DaveBurgessConsulting.com/DBCIbooks**.

More from the *Like a PIRATE*™ Series

Teach Like a PIRATE by Dave Burgess

eXPlore Like a PIRATE by Michael Matera

Learn Like a PIRATE by Paul Solarz

Play Like a PIRATE by Quinn Rollins

Run Like a PIRATE by Adam Welcome

Tech Like a PIRATE by Matt Miller

Lead Like a PIRATE™ Series

Lead Like a PIRATE by Shelley Burgess and Beth Houf

Balance Like a PIRATE by Jessica Cabeen, Jessica Johnson, and Sarah Johnson

Lead beyond Your Title by Nili Bartley

Lead with Appreciation by Amber Teamann and Melinda Miller

Lead with Culture by Jay Billy

Lead with Instructional Rounds by Vicki Wilson

Lead with Literacy by Mandy Ellis

Leadership & School Culture

Beyond the Surface of Restorative Practices by Marisol Rerucha

Choosing to See by Pamela Seda and Kyndall Brown

Culturize by Jimmy Casas

Discipline Win by Andy Jacks

Escaping the School Leader's Dunk Tank by Rebecca Coda and Rick Jetter

Fight Song by Kim Bearden

From Teacher to Leader by Starr Sackstein

If the Dance Floor Is Empty, Change the Song by Joe Clark

The Innovator's Mindset by George Couros

It's OK to Say "They" by Christy Whittlesey

Kids Deserve It! by Todd Nesloney and Adam Welcome

Let Them Speak by Rebecca Coda and Rick Jetter

The Limitless School by Abe Hege and Adam Dovico

Live Your Excellence by Jimmy Casas

Next-Level Teaching by Jonathan Alsheimer

The Pepper Effect by Sean Gaillard

Principaled by Kate Barker, Kourtney Ferrua, and Rachael George

The Principled Principal by Jeffrey Zoul and Anthony McConnell

Relentless by Hamish Brewer

The Secret Solution by Todd Whitaker, Sam Miller, and Ryan Donlan

Start. Right. Now. by Todd Whitaker, Jeffrey Zoul, and Jimmy Casas

Stop. Right. Now. by Jimmy Casas and Jeffrey Zoul

Teachers Deserve It by Rae Hughart and Adam Welcome

Teach Your Class Off by CJ Reynolds

They Call Me "Mr. De" by Frank DeAngelis

Thrive through the Five by Jill M. Siler

Unmapped Potential by Julie Hasson and Missy Lennard

When Kids Lead by Todd Nesloney and Adam Dovico

Word Shift by Joy Kirr

Your School Rocks by Ryan McLane and Eric Lowe

Technology & Tools

50 Things to Go Further with Google Classroom by Alice Keeler and Libbi Miller

50 Things You Can Do with Google Classroom by Alice Keeler and Libbi Miller

140 Twitter Tips for Educators by Brad Currie, Billy Krakower, and Scott Rocco

Block Breaker by Brian Aspinall

Building Blocks for Tiny Techies by Jamila "Mia" Leonard

Code Breaker by Brian Aspinall

The Complete EdTech Coach by Katherine Goyette and Adam Juarez

Control Alt Achieve by Eric Curts

The Esports Education Playbook by Chris Aviles, Steve Isaacs, Christine Lion-Bailey, and Jesse Lubinsky

Google Apps for Littles by Christine Pinto and Alice Keeler

Master the Media by Julie Smith

Raising Digital Leaders by Jennifer Casa-Todd

Reality Bytes by Christine Lion-Bailey, Jesse Lubinsky, and Micah Shippee, PhD

Sail the 7 Cs with Microsoft Education by Becky Keene and Kathi Kersznowski

Shake Up Learning by Kasey Bell

Social LEADia by Jennifer Casa-Todd

Stepping Up to Google Classroom by Alice Keeler and Kimberly Mattina

Teaching Math with Google Apps by Alice Keeler and Diana Herrington

Teachingland by Amanda Fox and Mary Ellen Weeks

Teaching with Google Jamboard by Alice Keeler and Kimberly Mattina

Teaching Methods & Materials

All 4s and 5s by Andrew Sharos

Boredom Busters by Katie Powell

The Classroom Chef by John Stevens and Matt Vaudrey

The Collaborative Classroom by Trevor Muir

Copyrighteous by Diana Gill

CREATE by Bethany J. Petty

Ditch That Homework by Matt Miller and Alice Keeler

Ditch That Textbook by Matt Miller

Don't Ditch That Tech by Matt Miller, Nate Ridgway, and Angelia Ridgway

EDrenaline Rush by John Meehan

Educated by Design by Michael Cohen, The Tech Rabbi

The EduProtocol Field Guide by Marlena Hebern and Jon Corippo

The EduProtocol Field Guide: Book 2 by Marlena Hebern and Jon Corippo

The EduProtocol Field Guide: Math Edition by Lisa Nowakowski and Jeremiah Ruesch

Expedition Science by Becky Schnekser

Fully Engaged by Michael Matera and John Meehan

Game On? Brain On! by Lindsay Portnoy, PhD

Guided Math AMPED by Reagan Tunstall

Innovating Play by Jessica LaBar-Twomy and Christine Pinto

Instant Relevance by Denis Sheeran

Keeping the Wonder by Jenna Copper, Ashley Bible, Abby Gross, and Staci Lamb

LAUNCH by John Spencer and A.J. Juliani

Make Learning MAGICAL by Tisha Richmond

Pass the Baton by Kathryn Finch and Theresa Hoover

Project-Based Learning Anywhere by Lori Elliott

Pure Genius by Don Wettrick

The Revolution by Darren Ellwein and Derek McCoy

Shift This! by Joy Kirr

Skyrocket Your Teacher Coaching by Michael Cary Sonbert

Spark Learning by Ramsey Musallam

Sparks in the Dark by Travis Crowder and Todd Nesloney

Table Talk Math by John Stevens

Unpack Your Impact by Naomi O'Brien and LaNesha Tabb

The Wild Card by Hope and Wade King

The Writing on the Classroom Wall by Steve Wyborney

You Are Poetry by Mike Johnston

Inspiration, Professional Growth & Personal Development

Be REAL by Tara Martin

Be the One for Kids by Ryan Sheehy

The Coach ADVenture by Amy Illingworth

Creatively Productive by Lisa Johnson

Educational Eye Exam by Alicia Ray

The EduNinja Mindset by Jennifer Burdis

Empower Our Girls by Lynmara Colón and Adam Welcome

Finding Lifelines by Andrew Grieve and Andrew Sharos

The Four O'Clock Faculty by Rich Czyz

How Much Water Do We Have? by Pete and Kris Nunweiler

P Is for Pirate by Dave and Shelley Burgess

A Passion for Kindness by Tamara Letter

The Path to Serendipity by Allyson Apsey

Sanctuaries by Dan Tricarico

Saving Sycamore by Molly B. Hudgens

The SECRET SAUCE by Rich Czyz

Shattering the Perfect Teacher Myth by Aaron Hogan

Stories from Webb by Todd Nesloney

Talk to Me by Kim Bearden

Teach Better by Chad Ostrowski, Tiffany Ott, Rae Hughart, and Jeff Gargas

Teach Me, Teacher by Jacob Chastain

Teach, Play, Learn! by Adam Peterson

The Teachers of Oz by Herbie Raad and Nathan Lang-Raad

TeamMakers by Laura Robb and Evan Robb

Through the Lens of Serendipity by Allyson Apsey

The Zen Teacher by Dan Tricarico

Children's Books

Beyond Us by Aaron Polansky

Cannonball In by Tara Martin

Dolphins in Trees by Aaron Polansky

I Want to Be a Lot by Ashley Savage

The Princes of Serendip by Allyson Apsey

Ride with Emilio by Richard Nares

The Wild Card Kids by Hope and Wade King

Zom-Be a Design Thinker by Amanda Fox

Made in the USA
Monee, IL
10 February 2024

53271006R00115